Center for
Middle Eastern Studies

Center for
International Affairs

The Economy of Cyprus

A. J. Meyer

with Simos Vassiliou

Harvard University Press
Cambridge
1962

Distributed in Great Britain by Oxford University Press, London

Library of Congress Catalog Card Number 62–8183
Printed in the United States of America

Preface

Its quality aside, this book bears two undeniable distinctions. Its modest length — under a hundred pages — makes it a rarity in economic development literature. Next, it enters a world preoccupied with national economic goals and targets without itself setting forth a Five Year Development Plan for Cyprus. It is designed for the general reader, and the specialist in economics or economic planning should consult recent issues of the *Cyprus Economic Review* (produced under the direction of Mr. Vassiliou) or Professor Willard Thorp's *Cyprus: Suggestions for a Development Program* (United Nations, 1961).

The authors wrote the book for several reasons. Both are interested in Middle Eastern and Mediterranean economic development and feel that Cyprus — because it is small and more "manageable" than nearby overpopulated countries — could well become a laboratory for economic development and yield results useful elsewhere. Unlike nearby Israel (which has long aspired to laboratory status for the Middle East),

Cyprus has a social and economic structure not very different from that of several nations nearby. Its political and economic future is extremely interesting to England, the United Nations, and the Atlantic Alliance, and of course to Greece and Turkey. The Arab states, Israel, and Soviet Bloc countries are busily wooing the new Republic. Its economic health will most certainly influence its politics.

Another reason for the book is the appeal offered by Cyprus' tradition of undisturbed political continuity. British stewardship before 1960 (despite the troubles of the 1950's) left Cyprus a legacy of good roads, a high level of literacy, and strength in other elements of infrastructure that are appallingly weak in many nearby mainland countries. The new Republic does *not* have, for example, an entrenched landholding class to impede reforms of all kinds. Of interest to the economist, British rule also left Cyprus an admirable statistical record of the details of its economic life.

The availability of these statistical data made possible an input-output study of the economy of Cyprus, the results of which are presented in the Appendix. Mr. Vassiliou collected the statistical material while serving as Director of the Statistics Section of the Crown Colony's Financial Secretary's office, and completed his basic analysis in 1958–59, when in residence at Harvard University as Research Associate of the Center for International Affairs and of the Center for Middle Eastern Studies. The input-output study was designed to supplement more traditional analytic techniques (such as national income accounting) and to illuminate intersectoral buying and selling on the island. From it the authors gained a clearer view than would otherwise have been possible of the extent to which mutually complementary agricultural and industrial growth fed one another in Cyprus during the 1950's.

No effort is made in these pages to outline a development

program or to translate the input-output data into a linear programing model. An admirable start on a Five Year Plan, using more traditional techniques, has already been made by Professor Willard Thorp. The authors concur that until several basic problems — particularly water — are solved, and more sectoral linkage develops in the Cyprus economy, an involved input-output exercise (replete with coefficients of various kinds) would be of interest chiefly to its compilers. Our intent to date has been to use the technique as a tool in interpreting economic history.

In studying the recent economic history of Cyprus, the authors have been impressed by the extreme reliance on the outside world exhibited by the island's economy. Just as several Arab states and Iran run their governments and stoke their investments with oil earnings, and Israel meets its enormous import deficits with gifts from abroad and addition to its national debt, so Cyprus pays its way by selling its location as a cold war air base and, in lesser degree, by exporting minerals. Its economy, like that of many of its mainland neighbors, seems overdependent on outside forces beyond its control. Internal developments during the 1950's did little to lessen the dependence.

We wish to emphasize here, however, what the dull economic facts in these pages may on occasion obscure, namely, our inherent optimism about the economic future of independent Cyprus. Over time, we remind the reader, Cyprus has given the world two such unlike, and useful, commodities as love and copper ore. More recently it has established, amidst twentieth century secularism, a new theocratic state. Finally, it served, during the decade of the 1950's, as the incubator for the writings of Laurence Durrell. On such a record, it is hard to envision defeat. But much work, and much compromise, lie ahead.

The comments of many readers improved the manuscript. In particular, the authors are indebted to the following: Nancy Crawshaw, for many years *Manchester Guardian* correspondent for Cyprus; David Percival, a senior official of the Crown Colony during most of the two decades 1940–1960; Willard Depree, Economic Officer of the U.S. Consulate in Cyprus from 1958 to 1960; N. G. Dimitriou, businessman and industrialist of Larnaca; George Christofides, businessman of Nicosia; Mehmet Aziz, Member of the Public Service Commission, Government of Cyprus; Fraser Wilkins, first United States Ambassador to the Republic of Cyprus; Charles McCaskill of the United States Embassy staff; Professors H. A. R. Gibb and Wassily Leontief of Harvard University; Dr. Elizabeth Gilboy and Mr. D. W. Lockard of Harvard University; Professor Paul Dodd of the University of California; Dr. P. J. Dhrymes of the Massachusetts Institute of Technology.

Our thanks also to Miss Brenda Sens and Miss Carolyn Cross of the Center for Middle Eastern Studies for their help in the preparation of this manuscript.

All mistakes and errors in judgment are solely the responsibility of the authors.

A. J. Meyer
Simos Vassiliou

Nicosia, Cyprus
September 1961

Contents

Tables

Appendix Charts

(inside back cover)

The Economy of Cyprus

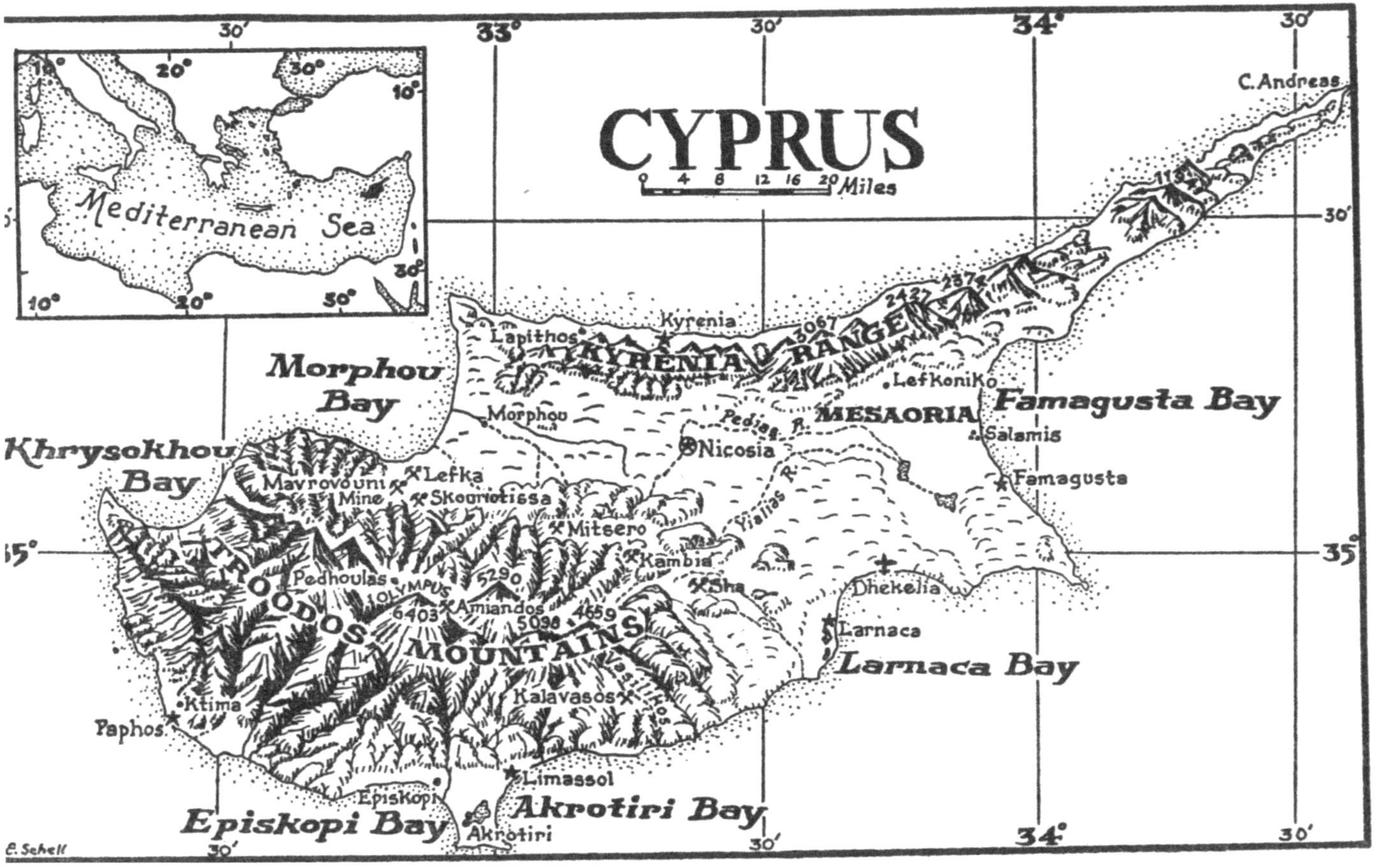
CYPRUS
0 4 8 12 16 20 Miles
Mediterranean Sea
C. Andreas
Kyrenia
Lapithos
KYRENIA RANGE
3067
2427
2374
Lefkoniko
Famagusta Bay
MESAORIA
Pedias R.
Salamis
Famagusta
Nicosia
Morphou
Morphou Bay
Khrysokhou Bay
Mavrovouni Mine
Lefka
Skouriotissa
Mitsero
Kambia
Sha
Yialias R.
Dhekelia
Larnaca
Larnaca Bay
TROODOS MOUNTAINS
Pedhoulas
OLYMPUS
6403
Amiandos
5290
5098
4659
Kalavasos
Vasili Kos
Ktima
Paphos
Limassol
Episkopi
Episkopi Bay
Akrotiri
Akrotiri Bay
33°
34°
35°
30′
E. Schell

1

Geography and Economic Setting

Cyprus is the most easterly island of consequence in the Mediterranean Sea. It is also the third largest island in that sea — only Sicily and Sardinia exceed it in size. Its 3,600 square miles of land make it roughly equal in area to Lebanon or Puerto Rico. On clear days the coastlines of Turkey and Syria may be seen from its shores. Lebanon and Israel lie only a few hours away by motor ship. In jet aircraft the flight to Suez takes less than an hour.

The island's main morphological features are its two mountain ranges, one in the north and the other in the southwest, surrounded by coastal and inland plains. The northern Kyrenia range is a limestone outcropping rising to about 3,000 feet. The southern Troodos range contains Mount Olympus, 6,400 feet above sea level, an igneous and limestone formation. Both ranges offer valleys convenient for motor roads.

The shoulders of the mountain ranges and the central plain which connects them, known as the Mesaoria, provide Cyprus its agricultural land — for citrus plantings along the sea, grapes and olive, carob, and deciduous fruit trees on the terraced hillsides, cereals on the flat expanses of the plain. Soils range from the terra rossa lands near Morphou Bay on the west to a grey alluvium through most of the rest of the island. There are several small rivers, such as the Yialias and Pedias. Others, as portrayed by sixteenth century mapmakers, at one time flowed into the sea and today create the alluvial fans on which rest four of of the island's six district towns.

Cyprus has the typical eastern Mediterranean variations of well defined summer and winter climates, with spring and autumn often indistinguishable as seasons. Winter brings occasional rains and traveling cyclones between spells of bright sunshine. Fog and drizzle are rare. Winter mean temperatures average from 50° to 55° throughout most of the island and from 30° to 36° in the higher mountains. Summers are hot and virtually rainless; mean temperatures in the lowland plains average in the low eighties and those in the mountains in the low seventies. Summers are humid along the coast and dry inland.

Rainfall is a constant problem. Cyprus lies just outside the eastern shore continental weather belt — where warm winter winds from Africa intersect with continental cold fronts to precipitate 35 to 40 inches of rain each year onto coastal Syria, Lebanon, and Israel. Only the high mountains of Cyprus get moisture in this amount — much of it as snow. Farming Cyprus is lucky to get 17 inches of rain, and 12 to 15 inches is more normal. As elsewhere in the Eastern Mediterranean, variations in rainfall occur with depressing regularity. Once in ten years the island suffers a really serious drought, and once in three a moderately serious one. The years 1957–1960 were marked by very low rainfall.

The island's geological structure enhances the water problem. The igneous and limestone formations of subsoil are porous, faulted, and seemingly perniciously designed by nature to assist the eroded topsoil in depositing far too much of the island's annual rainfall into the sea. Winter rains often create flash floods that run off immediately to the sea. In some areas fresh-water springs pour all year long into the sea offshore. Meanwhile pump irrigation is severely limited by the quantity of subsoil water. There are no major rivers with dams, and catchment basins on the hillsides for spring runoff mark the most successful conservation effort. Thus, with present techniques, less than 20 per cent of the island's rainfall is used by man, and only 6 per cent of its soil is irrigable.

Like much of the eastern Mediterranean, Cyprus is a living monument to man as a parasite on the soil. Beginning in the third millennium before Christ, the island's inhabitants worked with an uncalculated, yet skillful, rapacity to change the ecology and deplete the soil of the land. Mediterranean forests which once covered much of the island were hacked away at by the Phoenicians (selling cedar wood to the cabinetmakers of ancient Egypt), by the Greeks, Romans, Byzantines, and Ottomans, and more recently by the island's Greek and Turkish inhabitants. Somewhere along the line man was joined by that picturesque and playful symbol of a depraved agriculture, the goat. Together man and goat, cutting, burning, and grazing, have done a tragically effective job on Cyprus.

During the 1940's and 1950's, the Crown Colony's Forestry Department launched major programs of reforestation. By 1958, these had covered most of the high mountain areas and part of the foothills with indigenous trees — Aleppo and Troodos pine, Cyprus cedar, and Mediterranean cypress. These now join with degraded forest vegetation (such as thyme, prickly turnet, and garigue) to grow on almost 20 per cent of the island's land. But the eroded lowlands remain, and Cypriote farmers still pay for the destructive land-mining practices of their forebears.

The island's chief mineral and major exportable asset is copper ore. Production of copper still goes on in the Mavrovouni Mine, near Skouriotissa — one of the original sources of the world's copper. Since 1945 Cyprus has produced as much as one million tons of ore yearly, from which are extracted and sold abroad smaller quantities of refined copper, cupreous pyrites, and iron pyrites. Mines on the island also produce small quantities of asbestos and chrome ore.

Cyprus has other assets. One is its antiquities, archaeological excavation sites, and rich folklore. Artifacts from the neolithic age to Ottoman times have been, and are still being, dug from the island's soil. Greco-Roman temples and other ruins of minor repute are found throughout the island. The Greek goddess of love, Aphrodite, is generally believed to have been spawned in the sea foam on the island's beaches. While less exciting than the Acropolis, Karnak, or Persepolis, Cyprus offers much to interest the amateur as well as the professional antiquarian.

The island's location appeals to vacationers from the Middle East. Lebanese, Egyptians, and Israelis find Cyprus accessible and refreshing. So do American and British oil workers from the Persian Gulf on short leaves. Compared to Beirut, Tel Aviv, and Bahrein, most of Cyprus is deliciously cool in summer. Also it is "different" and, in the eyes of some, more "European" than the cities farther east. Several of the island's beaches are excellent by any standards.

Another advantage is the tradition of recent continuity afforded by the island's rulers. Britain ruled Cyprus for eighty years, until 1959 — Queen Victoria having taken over from the Ottoman sultan in 1878 as part of the horse-trading which punctuated the latter years of the "Eastern question" and Britain's nineteenth century efforts to check Russian expansion into the Middle East. In 1882, Britain adopted the legislative principle of government for Cyprus and appointed a council to advise the High Commissioner and a legislature with elected and appointed members. The latter body was enlarged in 1925, when the island was given status as a Crown colony.

Still another asset is Cyprus' value to Western military strategists. This value became evident during World War II, when the island served as airbase, refueling station for flights to the Far East, and support center for caique guerilla operations against Axis forces in Greece. After the war the island's importance multiplied with each new contraction westward of the British Empire. The evacuation of British forces from Suez made Cyprus the obvious headquarters for commando forces to combat disturbances on the Middle East mainland. During the Suez operations in 1956, paratroop battalions launched flights from the island. Since 1940, United Kingdom military expenditures have been the economic life blood of Cyprus.

The people of Cyprus are also an asset. There are now about 577,000 inhabitants, with a moderate (on Middle Eastern standards) population density of about 160 persons per square mile. About 80 per cent of Cypriotes are of Greek extraction, just under 20 per cent are of Turkish lineage, and there are also small minorities of Armenians, Jews, Maronites, and Europeans. The annual birth rate of 26 per thousand inhabitants is high, and the death rate of 6 per thousand is one of the world's lowest. In the field of public health, Cyprus stands as a monument to successful efforts by a Western governing authority. Cursed with widespread malaria as recently as 1938, the island today is virtually free of the disease. Infant mortality has dropped from eighty deaths per thousand live births to less than thirty-three since only 1945. The net population increase averages about 1.75 per cent yearly. Since World War II, the population distribution has been about 60 per cent rural and 40 per cent urban. Most of the city dwellers live in the six district towns — Nicosia, Kyrenia, Limassol, Famagusta, Larnaca, and Paphos — and their level of literacy is close to 80 per cent.

Added to the inventory of physical and human resources is a set of mental attitudes and capacities more difficult to define. Cypriotes, for one thing, are mobile. Factory owners, builders, and operators of military establishments have invariably found a pool of willing workers in the island's villages. Unlike many nearby Middle Easterners, Cypriotes seem willing to stay with factory jobs from the onset. They are quite willing to go abroad, and each year from 3,500 to 4,500 Cypriotes emigrate — most go to England, Australia, and Africa. In 1960, more than 12,000 Cypriotes emigrated. Many prove extremely successful in overseas pursuits. Further, in the troubles with Britain over Enosis, Cypriotes displayed attitudes noteworthy for their lack of docile acquiescence. As one resident put it, "Virtually overnight they changed their view toward Britain from that of a benevolent old nanny to one of cunning colonial oppressor."

The extent to which the physical and intellectual vigor of Cypriotes represents a pool of entrepreneurial talent is debatable. Several factories and many commercial establishments on the island are well run, aggressive, and financially successful. In each of the six district towns there is a group of businessmen who are well educated and highly sophisticated. But most Cypriote merchants either import, or deal in, foreign-made goods. No Cypriote merchant or banker is really a force — as are dozens of Lebanese — in the lucrative East-

West entrepôt trade. The island's real marks in international trade have come through copper exports — which are handled almost entirely by foreigners. Yet "other-worldliness" or lack of greed does not seem to hinder the Cypriote enterpriser. Like nearby Israel and Lebanon, Cyprus offers evidence to prove (and confound) exponents of almost every theory of entrepreneurial motivation.

Rural Cyprus likewise is replete with contradictions for the economic development theorist. Many of the island's villages are admittedly pretty bleak places. Yet the response of rural Cypriotes to city job opportunities since 1940 has been anything but apathetic. The growing statistics of education and literacy testify to real vigor. So do the numbers of Cypriotes who earn higher degrees abroad (there are no colleges or universities on the island) and who stay abroad to make real marks for themselves. Undeniably the island's economy has gained much from the occasional bright young man — educated abroad — who returns to play an important role in business or government.

Colonial rule has obviously influenced the economic mentality of the Cypriotes. The Ottomans, as stewards prior to 1878, granted fiefs and concessions to Ottoman functionaries and installed the Turkish component of the population — which today has declined to 18 per cent. The beys in Constantinople obviously saw Cyprus as part of their scheme of empire, not as home of a people whose uplift was the proprietor's duty. For much of the period of Ottoman rule, there is little evidence that Turkey had other than the mildest of clinical interest in the island.

To a much lesser extent, the same could be said about Britain's interest prior to World War II. During World War I, for example, England offered to cede Cyprus to Greece. The latter refused the gift, thus joining England and Turkey on the list of nations whose interest in Aphrodite's isle could be termed less than vibrant. With the advent of demands by Cypriotes for union with Greece in the 1930's — distinguished by the burning of the governor's mansion — the Colonial Office rescinded the legislative aspects of rule on Cyprus. From then until the London and Zurich agreements of 1959, which paved the way for the island to become a republic, Cyprus was ruled by governors responsible solely to the Colonial Office. An executive council advised the governor and, in years of tranquillity, contained Cypriotes as members. With the crescendo of Enosis — the movement for union with Greece — after 1955, however, Cypriotes had in fact virtually nothing to do with political policy making.

Colonial Office rule of Cyprus before 1940 emphasized honest administration. Above all, it ensured that each unit of the empire paid its own way and was not a financial burden on England. Cyprus accomplished this by selling its minerals abroad in the depressed world copper and pyrites markets. A series of governors (among them Sir Ronald Storrs) were, on the whole, men of ability. The Crown Colony government ran administrations which lacked venality and corruption and, on standards of the time, governed Cyprus well. In a world which had not yet invented the Marshall and Colombo plans — and which was only mildly concerned with national income accounting — Britain's between-wars stewardship of Cyprus may be described as essentially benign.

2

Expansion and Problems, 1943–1960

Relatively little of actual fact is known about the economy of Cyprus prior to World War II. The colonial administration conducted censuses of population every ten years after 1881 and kept good records of imports and exports. But no figures exist on levels of national income, currency transactions, investment, or the other data which are now almost household terms in the parlance of those concerned with developing nations. With its pound tied to sterling, Cyprus was part of the great free-trading area whose nerve center lay in the London money market. Except for its role as a small-scale exporter of copper ore and cupreous and iron pyrites, most of which went to smelters on the Continent, Cyprus was unimportant both to the world economy and to the arena of political and military strategy. After Greece refused Cyprus as a gift, Britain probably kept it largely as insurance against future troubles unforeseen.

These of course came during the years 1939–1945. The Middle East's actual and its expected involvement in the war put the island into a role in world affairs more crucial than it had played since ancient times. It became, as the war progressed, a take-off point for Allied guerillas working with the underground in Greece. As Rommel's desert corps swept eastward across North Africa, Cyprus became part of the network of harassment bases planned to plague German forces should they overrun Cairo and move northward into Palestine, Lebanon, and Syria.

Economically to Cyprus the war meant air base construction, extensive improvement of public health conditions, and a transfusion of quantities of money via the pockets of soldiers quartered on the island. It also meant controls of all kinds — administered by the Middle East Supply Centre in Cairo as part of Britain's task of feeding the area and regulating its economic relations. Some privation was felt by upper-income Cypriotes as German torpedoes made luxury goods from abroad scarce, but to most Cypriotes the war meant more jobs, much better income, and relief from the drab monotony of life in the island's villages. Even those Cypriotes who drilled with the Cyprus Volunteer Force took it lightheartedly. The six district towns burgeoned as service centers for the British military establishment.

After the war a series of developments joined not only to prevent economic collapse but to push the island's economy to ever higher levels. The first of these was the British decision to withdraw from Palestine and the subsequent creation of Israel by the United Nations. Once this was done, Britain's strategists came increasingly to view Cyprus as a new police station, to be used with Suez bases to quell disturbances certain to come in the Levant. Investment in bases was stepped up.

Further support for the "police station" concept came with the granting of independence to India and Pakistan, the beginnings of pressure by Egypt for withdrawal of British forces from the canal zone, the emergence of three Arab states and Iran as major suppliers of petroleum to Europe's expanding market, and the construction of pipelines linking Iraq and the Persian Gulf with the eastern Mediterranean. The actual withdrawal of Britain from Suez in 1952 — by which time almost three million barrels of Middle Eastern oil was moving westward daily — climaxed the debate in favor of the military. From then until 1958, transfers from the United Kingdom Treasury each year for base construction on Cyprus moved steadily upward.

So too did the island's earnings from mineral shipments after 1945. Before the war these had meant little. The Cyprus Mines Corporation, an American firm working ore seams near Skouriotissa, had operated since 1905, but world mineral prices were low between the wars and tax royalty payments to the Crown Colony were modest. During the 1920's and 1930's, and immediately after World War II, the Cyprus Mines Corporation invested heavily in plant and mine facilities, hoping for a price upturn. This came with the snowballing momentum of European postwar economic recovery. Copper soared for a while after 1950 to fifty cents a pound. Prices of cupreous and iron pyrites rose proportionately. By then the mines were producing some 800,000 tons of 5 per cent ore yearly, creating jobs for several thousand Cypriotes and pumping a further transfusion into the island's system of public works.

Cyprus also benefited from the Korean war. Shortages of goods and shipping space proved an aid to local industry on the island and permitted it to consolidate the gains it had made during and after World War II, largely through import-substitution to lower-income consumers. Germany had not by that time again become a major exporter, and British goods were preferred by upper-income Cypriotes. The island's small industries gained renewed momentum during the Asian debacle.

Postwar prosperity on Cyprus was also fed by an increasing flow of emigrant remittances and by growing earnings from tourism. Each of these sources accounted for at least $10 million yearly prior to 1955. By the latter year, political disturbances and military curfews joined to discourage tourism. But gifts to islanders from overseas relatives — mostly resident in the United Kingdom or British empire — accounted for almost $20 per Cypriote yearly for most of the decade. Before 1955 (as again since 1960) tourism did the same.

Of interest to the economist in all this was a decision by the Colonial Office to strengthen its hitherto virtually nonexistent program of statistics collection and to begin measuring economic change on the island. The first economic survey was made in 1950. Since that time the details of the island's economy have become known with increasing clarity. Details of sterling area transactions (before the war largely unknown because of the lack of controls), national income figures, balance of payments charts, industrial censuses, estimates of investment and capital formation, commercial censuses — all are now made public, in great detail, at regular intervals. Cyprus is one of the few so-called underdeveloped countries where statistical data for a reasonably accurate measurement of change are now available.*

By usual indicators, that change has been rapid and upward. National income estimates, for example, portray a rapid increase in the island's net product since 1950. In that year Cyprus produced a national income of just over $100 million, about $200 per capita. By 1957 the national income had more than doubled, soaring over $200 million, $400 per capita. In-

* See the recent issues of the *Cyprus Economic Review*.

flation of 54 per cent during the period and population growth totaling about 12 per cent cut the net per capita income advance to over 3.5 per cent yearly — still a rapid rate of expansion. Numerically Cyprus has come close to the net rates of per capita advance posted by Israel from 1948 to 1958, by Syria from 1947 to 1955, by Lebanon from 1949 to 1957, and by Greece in the last two years. While its rate of climb in recent years has lagged behind those of several European countries, it has exceeded the average rates of most countries in the Western world since 1800.

Investment, too, has gone on at an extraordinarily high rate. In 1950, the Crown Colony and Cypriote private investors ploughed in about $15 million, 15 per cent of the net national income. By 1957 they were investing over $50 million yearly, 27 per cent of net national income. Approximately 20 per cent of the investment consisted of public funds and 80 per cent of private funds. These figures denote a very high rate of capital formation, compare favorably with investment rates in Israel and Lebanon, and exceed by far those registered in most other countries of the world.

Deficits in balances of trade likewise go upward — a fact which worries some, yet which others see as the mark of healthy and vigorous economy. The difference between purchases abroad and sales abroad grew from about $11 million in 1951 to over $55 million in 1959. In themselves the deficits mean little, for they were covered over the eight year period by United Kingdom Treasury transfers to the island for military base expansion and troop quartering. In effect the transfers both created and paid for the trading deficits.

Indeed, United Kingdom Treasury transfers to Cyprus since 1950 have given dominant motive force to the island's economic expansion. These, spent approximately 50 per cent on works expenditure (construction materials, labor, machinery), 15 per cent on civilian pay (to British and Cypriotes), 25 per cent on servicemen's pay for local spending, and 10 per cent on direct service expenditures other than works, have risen markedly. The tabulation below shows the total transfers from 1952 to 1960:

	£ Million	*$ Million*
1952	4.16	11.6
1953	4.33	12.12
1954	6.73	18.84
1955	10.10	28.28
1956	20.31	56.86
1957	21.00	58.80
1958	21.32	59.69
1959	19.87	55.64
1960	20.18	56.50

A reasonable estimate of the impact on Cyprus' economy of transfers from the United Kingdom Treasury may be made for 1957. In that year, funds and equipment worth almost $60 million were made available. Of this, an estimated $15 million consisted of British machinery and construction materials. The remaining $45 million accounted for at least eight thousand jobs for Cypriotes directly associated with jobs on bases and for eight to ten thousand jobs for those indirectly associated with base activities — contractors building flats designed for occupancy by dependents, and so on. In addition the funds most certainly had a multiplier effect throughout the economy. While impossible to estimate with accuracy, this could have accounted for several thousand jobs also. In all, as many as twenty thousand jobs were involved — almost 40 per cent of the nonagricultural labor force of the island.

Another big impetus came from expanded ore production after 1950 and increased exports of cupreous and iron pyrites.

Ore production grew from about 800,000 tons in 1951 to over 1,350,000 tons in 1960. The value of mineral exports grew meanwhile, triggered by soaring world copper and pyrites prices, to a peak of about $33 million in 1956. Of this, some $4–$5 million was paid in wages to the 4,000 mine workers, $10–$12 million was paid to the Crown Colony Government as royalty and income tax on earnings, and the remainder went to cover non-wage operating costs and company profits. Mineral exports, in short, created about 4,000 jobs yearly and paid about a quarter of the Crown Colony's ordinary governmental operating expenses over the period in question.

As will be shown in later chapters, industry, agriculture, and tourism on Cyprus likewise expanded during the years under scrutiny. In industry, the big gains were made by construction. More farmland was irrigated. Until 1955 the servicing of tourists was a lucrative and growing enterprise. But all of these were dwarfed in importance by the growth in national product attributable to trade and commerce. Like many other underdeveloped countries, Cyprus' initial response to enlarged capital transfers and purchasing power was to increase its imports of foreign-made goods and improve its arrangements for handling them. The commercial and services sector grew until it was by 1957 producing almost half the island's national income.

The foregoing testifies to statistical growth of substantial proportions during the years when Cyprus has employed the standard economic measuring rods. Yet beneath the record of growth lies a series of economic problems of a critical nature.

The first of these is the excessive reliance of Cyprus on international disaster and tension as a motive force for economic growth. Admittedly public expenditures on military matters are now important to the civil economies of most nations. War-induced shortages likewise influence the economic health of nations. But in Cyprus the reliance is extreme. In recent years United Kingdom transfers for military purposes have touched $60 million yearly — a figure equal to 25 per cent of the island's national income. Too many jobs and too great a proportion of investment depend on maintenance of military transfers. As though to accent the reliance, the island's national income dropped, between 1957 and 1960, a total of 12.7 per cent — largely in response to cuts in military expenditure.

Cyprus' value to the Western military establishment, furthermore, is far from immutable. Many strategists consider the island unimportant for a shooting war, but useful in a shouting war — as a police station for troops needed for small-scale, nonnuclear military operations in the Middle East. But even this concept has its critics — those who point to the embarrassing several-day interlude between the launching of the Suez operation by Britain, France, and Israel and the actual arrival of the sea-borne landing craft from Malta. Air-borne commandos flew from Cyprus, but the launching of even a small-scale surface attack from the island was impossible. As improvement in jet aircraft shrink distances even further, continental bases for air-borne commandos may serve Western military needs as well as island bases.

Cyprus also seems excessively dependent on its minerals as a generator of employment and source of tax revenue. Copper and pyrites experienced a ten-year price rise after 1945. As the minerals rose in price, 4,000 workers earned a good living producing it, and the $9–$10 million in tax-royalty just about covered the Crown Colony's annual investments in public works. But by 1957 price corrections occurred owing to overproduction in the world coupled with competitive inroads made by other metals, particularly aluminum and stainless steel. For several years since 1957, copper has sold at as low as half the postwar highs, occasionally dropping to twenty-five cents a pound. Pyrites prices fell proportionately. The cuts were reflected in decreased payments to the government of Cyprus and in decreased employment as companies mechanized to cut production costs. The island's high-grade (5 per cent) ore lodes were mined, moreover, rapidly toward exhaustion during the 1950's. By 1961 the Cyprus Mines Corporation was working lower-grade seams almost exclusively.

Still another problem relates to the distribution of income in Cyprus and the resultant narrowness of the domestic market. The urban middle class in Cyprus enjoys a per capita income well above the all-island average of $400. But over half the island's 577,000 inhabitants live from agriculture and exist on a per capita income nearer to $200. Such lopsided distribution undeniably promotes investment by middle-class, urban Cypriotes. But it has joined with many factors, discussed later, to check investment in the island's farmland. And it has helped prevent the inception of mutually complementary revolutions linking factories to farmers.

The pattern of investment in Cyprus accents the above problem and itself poses difficulties of great magnitude. Over the years 1953–1958, investment each year went roughly 50 per cent into construction (with upper-income urban housing taking the bulk of funds), 10 per cent into transportation (mainly passenger cars), 31 per cent into machinery and other producers' goods, and 5 per cent into plantations and mines. Investment in the island's two main pillars of sustenance — agriculture and mining — has been tiny, too low in producers' goods and transport (most developing nations have, over time, put about 22 per cent of net investment into transport improvements), and probably excessive in luxury housing. The inevitable conclusion is that far too little investment has gone into channels creating long-run employment and economic growth.

Part of the above problem, certainly not all, derives from still another hurdle which Cyprus must cross — that of a need for effective entrepreneurs and managers at all levels of the productive process. The family firm still dominates enterprise on the island; enterprise is almost wholly a risktaking proposition and has shown little of the vigor of its science-oriented counterpart in the Western world; most really successful "factories" on Cyprus are devoted to the manufacture of alcoholic beverages and soda pop; over the centuries Cyprus businessmen have been successful largely as middlemen and importers; so far not a single manufactured product from Cyprus has established itself as competitively superior in international trading.

Another problem which is too often glossed over is that related to the shortage of resources on Cyprus and the technological gap which still prevents recent miraculous discoveries — in nuclear fission and the rest — from righting the balance. Cyprus is poor in resources. Except for location, climate, and low grade copper ore, the island has scant resources to exploit. Water is a constant and ever pressing problem. Once Western technology makes irrigation flow from sea water economically practicable and plant-breeding produces improved grasses for the island's parched soil, real improvement might be felt. But the limitations placed on lasting growth by resource shortages can never be discounted.

The final problem plaguing Cyprus is that attendant upon the virtually imperceptible shift in the structure of the island's economy. One analysis, described in the Appendix, has measured the extent to which agriculture, industry, and commerce have changed roles as producers of the island's wealth. The study measured changes between 1954 and 1957 — years of great over-all expansion in national income. A sobering conclusion was reached. Discussion of these sectoral interrelationships is the concern of the chapters that follow.

3

Agriculture

Farming is the backbone of Cyprus' economy. Although mining, commercial activities, and manufacturing have shown more dramatic change in the past decade, most Cypriotes still draw their sustenance from agriculture. More than half of the gainfully employed persons on the island work full time at farming. And they produce about a quarter of Cyprus' national income.

As elsewhere in the Middle East, the social unit of agricultural Cyprus is the village. Of the island's slightly more than six hundred villages, a few have populations ranging from 2,000 to 6,000; most, however, have fewer than 1,000. Many villagers work in the district towns during the week and return home on weekends and holidays — thus imparting a fluidity to Cyprus' rural life rare in peasant societies.

By the most optimistic estimates, there are available to Cypriote farmers about one million cultivable acres, or slightly less than two acres per capita for the population as a whole. Such estimates include marginal land of varying quality, however, and a more realistic estimate of the island's cultivable acreage would probably be about 800,000. Given the island's rainfall, soil condition, and geological structure, the figure of one and a half acres per Cypriote — while high on Asian standards — does not permit affluence for the farmers.

Dry farming predominates. All but 15 per cent of the island's farmland is dependent upon rainfall watering, and is limited, therefore, almost exclusively to the production of cereal crops and carob pods. The irrigable 15 per cent includes land which is perennially irrigable (6 per cent of the farmland, mostly from pump wells) and that which is occasionally irrigable (about 9 per cent of the land) through control of flash-flood runoff.

Impressive measures by the British colonial administration after 1946 made possible the present ratios of irrigated to dry farming land. Cyprus has, for example, no year-round rivers worthy of the name. Scarcely a dozen streams run for two or three months a year, carrying melted snow and spate flood runoff. The government has installed facilities to utilize part of this water, as well as to tap the mountain springs with year-round flow. Chain-wells (underground cavities connected by man-made tunnels), a device widely used throughout the eastern Mediterranean in Roman times, have also been improved in recent years. Drilling of pump wells has also gone on at an accelerated pace, and the island is now believed to have about reached the limit of deep wells supportable by its underground water table. Yet despite these advances, no more than 20 per cent of the island's rainfall is used by man for farming, drinking, or industrial purposes.

Like soils elsewhere in the Mediterranean basin, those of Cyprus reflect long exploitation by man and goat — with resultant widespread alkalinity and low organic content. Light-colored, greyish Rendzina soils are widespread, as are heavy red soils known as terra rossas. The best farmland lies on the floodplains and coastal regions — alluvium deposited through centuries of erosion of mountain land. There are also carbonate and silicate raw soils and some areas of brown earths. Whatever their chemical makeup, the soils of Cyprus are almost universally too thin, rest on porous rock which absorbs rainfall with sponge-like efficiency, and are lacking in plant nutrients. Large areas known as "kafkalla" lands have been eroded completely bare of topsoil and today consist of only a hard calcareous layer of stonelike consistency.

Cyprus' principal crops are wheat and barley and vetches, grown on the Mesaoria plain with winter rainfall and occasional supplementary irrigation. Other spring crops are cotton, chick peas, sesame, and tobacco. Citrus fruits, grapes, olives, almonds, and carobs grow on the coastal plains and low mountain shoulders. The citrus fruits depend entirely upon irrigation.

The effects of continuous overcropping and erosion of cereal land are illustrated dramatically by the acreage and output figures for the past half-century. As shown in Table 1, yield per acre declined steadily from 1900 to 1949. Extension of citrus and deciduous fruit tree plantings during the 1940's took some of the better wheat land and hence distorts the figures somewhat, but the trend was definitely downward — as fewer bushels per acre resulted and as marginal land was put to the plow. The figures also reveal a dramatic upturn after 1950, as the Crown Colony government launched a fertilizer-import and soil-improvement program. These improvements pushed yields during 1950–1959 up to 15 per cent over the 1900–1909 decade and to 47 per cent above the 1940–1949 decade.

In terms of dry-land bushels per acre, Cyprus' cereal yield now compares most favorably with other so-called underdeveloped areas. Its wheat and oats output now exceeds fifteen

TABLE 1

Average annual production of cereals, by decades, 1900–1959

Decade	Wheat			Barley			Oats			All Cereals		
	Tons	Acres	Tons per acre	Tons	Acres	Tons per acre	Tons	Acres	Tons per acre	Tons	Acres	Tons per acre
1900–1909	51,382	—	—	51,830	—	—	5,605	—	—	108,817	—	—
1910–1919	53,351	—	—	43,753	—	—	6,146	—	—	103,250	—	—
1920–1929	54,071	180,351	0.300	42,400	113,909	0.372	3,465	14,341	0.242	99,936	308,601	0.324
1930–1939	50,058	182,277	.275	39,219	111,230	.353	3,558	11,708	.304	92,835	305,215	.304
1940–1949	44,732	192,838	.232	37,804	125,085	.302	2,579	11,683	.221	85,115	329,606	.258
1950–1959	63,586	191,120	.333	59,008	138,242	.427	2,436	9,156	.266	125,030	338,518	.369

bushels per acre and its barley yield is slightly higher. But these figures require downward adjustment because of the fallow system of farming which permits a crop only once every eighteen months or two years.

Grape raising ranks just behind cereal farming in importance to Cyprus agriculture. The area planted to vines is second only to wheat and barley, and an estimated twenty thousand families, almost 20 per cent of the population, derive their livelihood, in one way or another, from the grape. The island's total grape production in recent years has amounted to the following: 1953, 89,000 tons; 1954, 74,511; 1955, 86,562; 1956, 82,500; 1957, 82,424; 1958, 68,750; 1959, 128,750; 1960, 102,500. Part of the crop is used for raisins: from 1954 to 1957 raisin production averaged 6,800 tons annually; it dropped to 1,826 tons in 1958, then climbed to 8,660 tons in 1959 and 9,375 tons in 1960.

In ancient and early modern times, Cyprus was renowned for its wines. Indeed, the Ottoman conquest of the island in 1570 is often attributed to the overpowering thirst of Sultan Selim. In later Ottoman times, wine production on Cyprus dropped — possibly because of the puritanism of nineteenth century Ottoman functionaries. Britain, as the next proprietor, did not at first encourage plantings. But in the 1890's, when France's vineyards were destroyed by the phylloxera blight, Cypriotes were again encouraged to increase wine production. Widespread planting, using California seedlings for the most part, went on throughout the island on mountain terraces and coastal shoulders.

Authorities on wine express doubts that Cyprus can, or ever did, produce sizable quantities of dry table wines remotely comparable to the better vintages of France, the Rhine valley, or parts of Italy. The island's climate is too hot and dry, its growers and vintners did not, until very recently, develop the traditions of knowledge and loving concern which go with making fine wines, and it is said that Cyprus' dry wines do not travel as well as those from the continent. The result has been that Cyprus' dry wines are either consumed locally, sold in the eastern Mediterranean (usually in Egypt) to lower-income buyers, or shipped to Europe for mixing and sale with locally produced *vin ordinaire.*

The best Cyprus wines are those made from the sweeter grapes which elsewhere in the Mediterranean go into ports and sherries. In recent years, a semisweet vintage known as "commandaria" has gained widespread acceptance in the United Kingdom and on the Continent. Cyprus sherries also are exported — again mainly to Beirut and Cairo.

During the 1940's Crown Colony chemists and Cypriote wine producers conducted experiments which led the way to increased production of stronger beverages — aged brandies and anise-flavored *ouzo.* Production during World War II went largely to satisfy the tastes of British troops in the Middle East. After the war an export trade in ten-year-old brandy developed and flourished with little competition for a decade — until French cognacs re-entered the market in quantity. Recent statistics on the production of wine and spirits are given in Table 2.

Cyprus farmers have also shifted increasingly to production of table grapes since 1950. This came partially from the results of experiments by government agriculturists which proved that Cyprus grapes could compete successfully in United Kingdom markets, shielded by imperial preference arrangements. It also stemmed from the establishment of a series of highly modern grape plantations and packing facilities. These "factories in the fields" were partially Cypriote-owned and were partially directed and financed by Jewish interests in Israel.

The most startling agricultural increase in Cyprus during

TABLE 2

Production of wine and spirits, 1954–1960 (imperial gallons)

Year	Commandaria	Other wines	Spirits
1954	101,538	2,655,710	714,177
1955	265,824	2,567,988	604,263
1956	158,688	2,666,052	752,925
1957	118,440	2,353,104	790,477
1958	180,108	3,250,980	400,372
1959	395,546	3,850,900	979,375
1960	175,000	3,000,000	400,000

recent years has taken place in citrus plantings. Chiefly as a result of successful well drilling near Famagusta and Morphou, import preferences in United Kingdom markets, and improvement in production and grading techniques, output of oranges and lemons increased ten times between 1933 and 1958, from 31 million to 310 million. Jaffa and Valencia oranges are grown near Famagusta and Morphou, and lemons in the more sheltered areas near Lapithos in the north. Citrus acreage now totals about 40,000, and its productivity of 70–80 boxes per acre compares favorably with that in nearby Lebanon and Israel.

Like most other Mediterranean peoples, Cypriotes grow olive trees on mountain slopes and hillsides. In recent years grafted plantings have increased. Although almost every peasant owns a few trees, the output is so unpredictable — because of capricious rainfall — that only in rare years can the island supply its own needs of oil and pickled olives. The figures in Table 3 illustrate the wide fluctuations in output.

Carob trees are intermixed with olive plantings in many parts of Cyprus. Indigenous to the eastern Mediterranean, the carob tree is a hardy evergreen which thrives under the

TABLE 3

Production of olives and olive oil, 1949–1960 (tons)

Year	Olives	Olive oil[a]
1949	20,945	3,906
1950	9,779	1,695
1951	6,173	930
1952	11,082	2,117
1953	13,562	2,379
1954	7,889	1,263
1955	7,858	1,256
1956	12,710	2,382
1957	10,113	1,635
1958	6,220	1,010
1959	8,101	1,283
1960	6,250	625

[a] From 1909 to 1917 the annual average was 197 tons.

same growing conditions as olives. Its pods are exported to England for cattle feed, and, as Table 4 shows, production figures reveal considerable fluctuations, albeit milder than those besetting other crops in Cyprus.

In addition to the field and tree crops discussed above, Cypriotes each year produce a wide range of plants and fruits and vegetables of less importance. Among these are tobacco, anise, and sesame seeds, market vegetables of various kinds, deciduous-tree fruits such as apples and pears, and bananas, almonds, and walnuts. Together the acreage devoted to such products totals only about 5 per cent of the island's farm land, the output is mostly consumed locally, and the role of the crops is not great. In recent years potato production has increased and new potatoes are now exported.

Animal crop agriculture as practiced on Cyprus typifies a

TABLE 4

Production of carobs, 1931/32–1959/60[a] (thousands of tons)

1931/32	60.0	1946/47	47.5
1932/33	34.4	1947/48	44.8
1933/34	26.2	1948/49	39.9
1934/35	34.1	1949/50	44.8
1935/36	40.7	1950/51	45.3
1936/37	39.1	1951/52	52.1
1937/38	54.9	1952/53	38.9
1938/39	45.7	1953/54	54.1
1939/40	51.1	1954/55	50.0
1940/41	38.1	1955/56	50.3
1941/42	22.6	1956/57	45.7
1942/43	39.6	1957/58	46.5
1943/44	38.4	1958/59	53.0
1944/45	52.0	1959/60	42.1
1945/46	42.5		

[a] September to August.

central farm problem. All but a small percentage of Cypriotes' sheep and goats are owned by landless farmers, village butchers, town businessmen, or monasteries. Wheat and fruit farmers almost never own more than a few pigs and a sheep or two, and the raising of animals and animal feed in rotation with cereals is rare. Indiscriminate grazing of marginal lands has accompanied this arrangement for a century, with resultant ecological change and soil erosion. And the Cyprus wheat farmer has never enjoyed the sheet anchor of soil improvement and cash-crop diversification afforded by mixed farming elsewhere in the world.

Except for sheep, the animal population of Cyprus has dropped steadily since 1940, and sharply since 1955. Camels, as elsewhere in the Middle East, are being replaced by the motor truck; Cyprus mules, long famous in Turkey and Iran for their great stamina, have also been replaced by trucks; horses and dual-purpose cattle have diminished because of lack of forage and mechanical competition; and the island's pigs were decimated by epidemics.

Sheep alone have increased on Cyprus since 1900. This has been partially due to improvement of the Awasi and Karaman fat-tailed breeds common to the island, partially to grazing restrictions imposed by the government against goats, and partially to rising demand from the towns for lamb and mutton and hides and wool. But the increase has been insufficient to fill local meat needs, and meat prices on the island have risen much more rapidly than other foodstuffs in the past decade. Tables 5, 6, and 7 illustrate the decline in animal population since 1900.

Land tenure and usage rival water as the most serious problem facing Cyprus agriculture. Historically, Cypriote farmers, Greek and Turk alike, have divided their land according to Islamic and Ottoman land decrees. These called for division of land among several surviving heirs, with resultant over-fragmentation. Recent economic growth, while creating more

TABLE 5

Average annual animal population, by decades, 1900–1959

	1900–1909	1910–1919	1920–1929	1930–1939	1940–1949	1950–1959
Sheep	247,587	271,131	274,015	293,247	305,434	355,581
Goats	248,152	232,674	221,706	215,503	188,528	158,342
Pigs	37,877	35,745	34,847	30,701	36,408	33,566
Horses	—	—	3,825	4,366	4,450	3,303
Mules	—	—	7,003	9,290	10,160	6,999
Donkeys	—	—	45,330	53,142	56,582	44,803
Camels	—	—	1,238	1,054	836	309
Cattle	—	—	42,885	41,750	38,538	31,443

TABLE 6

Annual animal population since 1955

	1955	1956	1957	1958	1959
Sheep	382,240	385,210	381,130	394,260	406,580
Goats	147,350	157,860	158,720	132,410	144,580
Pigs	34,380	32,680	39,210	35,030	19,830
Horses	3,720	2,550	—	1,870	—
Mules	7,640	6,920	—	5,980	—
Donkeys	47,740	42,270	—	40,780	—
Camels	310	140	—	140	—
Cattle	34,720	28,410	—	31,340	—

non-farm occupations, has not really checked the process; nor did efforts of the colonial government, which were viewed with suspicion by villagers. By 1946, the land ownership pattern of Cyprus was as shown in Table 8. At that time, the average farm holding on the island was 19 acres, and 70 per cent of the island's farmers owned less than the average. By 1959, government agriculturists estimated that the average holding had shrunk to 15 acres — half of which lay fallow each year. Worse still, the holdings are often widely dispersed,

TABLE 7

Average number of animals per capita, by decades, 1900–1959

Decade	Sheep and goats	Pigs	Cattle
1900–1909	1.979	0.148	—
1910–1919	1.723	0.122	—
1920–1929	1.505	0.106	0.130
1930–1939	1.369	0.083	0.112
1940–1949	1.129	0.083	0.088
1950–1959	0.923	0.060	0.056

TABLE 8

Number of agricultural holdings of various sizes in 1946

Size in donums[a]	Number of holdings	Percentage of total number of holdings
Under 1	698	1.2
1–4	3,196	5.3
5–9	5,926	9.8
10–19	10,535	17.4
20–39	13,939	23.0
40–59	8,568	14.2
60–79	5,562	9.2
80–99	3,637	6.0
100–199	6,722	11.1
200–499	1,533	2.5
500–999	101	0.2
1000 and over	47	0.1

[a] 3.025 donums = one acre.

into an average of twelve plots per owner. Many farmers spend much of their working day bicycling or walking from plot to plot.*

A bright spot in the Cyprus land picture is the virtual absence of really exploitative — on Egyptian or Iranian standards — feudal and absentee ownership of holdings. Only some 7 per cent of the island's farmland is estimated to be in the hands of town-dwellers, and sharecropping is rare. The Cypriote farmer at least is still his own master. Many of the city farmers, moreover, are "improving landlords" whose operations are exploitative of neither the island's physical nor its human

* The best account of the land problem in Cyprus is that of Demetris Christodolou, *The Evolution of the Rural Land Use Pattern in Cyprus* (Bude, Cornwall, England, 1959).

resources. The city farmers have probably accounted for all but a fraction of the new private investment in Cyprus' agriculture in recent years.

The largest single landowner in Cyprus is the autocephalous Greek Orthodox Church. By outright purchase and through grants under wills the Church has come to control an estimated 8 to 10 per cent of the island's farmland. While no statistics on the subject are available, some observers feel that the Church lands include some of the island's best acreage. Most Church lands are rented, and every two years rents are established through village auctions. This system, by affording no guarantee of tenure, tends to discourage soil improvements by renters. The Moslem religious foundation, Evcaf, controls another 1 to 2 per cent of the island's farmland.

The cooperative movement has been a major force ameliorating the lot of the Cyprus peasant. It began in 1909 with a cooperative credit society in Lefkoniko, a wheat-producing village in the central Mesaoria. Today the movement comprises two central cooperative banks (one Greek and one Turkish), 864 cooperative societies of various kinds, and 700 school savings banks. The cooperatives' reserve funds now total more than $4 million, and the movement has clearly proved to be one of the more useful Western inventions imported into a Middle Eastern country.

Before 1936 cooperatives on Cyprus were under the Crown Colony Department of Agriculture. Since that date a separate government Department of Co-operative Development has promoted their growth — with the usual loans, tax exemptions, technical advice, and guarantees of various kinds. Cooperative offices now operate in most communities on the island, in a variety of fields.

Thrift and credit cooperatives are the oldest on Cyprus. Modeled after the original Lefkoniko Credit Society, these currently serve as funnels for rural savings, including those of school children, throughout the island. Between 1950 and 1958 their loans more than tripled (Table 9), and their deposits grew nearly fivefold, from $3.6 million to $17.6 million.

TABLE 9

Loans issued by cooperatives, 1950–1958 (millions of dollars)

Year	Short-term loans	Medium-term loans	Long-term loans	Total
1950	2.6	0.4	0.3	3.3
1951	3.4	0.4	0.3	4.1
1952	4.0	0.8	0.7	5.5
1953	5.1	0.4	0.5	6.0
1954	4.7	0.9	0.1	5.7
1955	5.5	1.2	0.1	6.8
1956	5.8	1.4	0.2	7.4
1957	9.1	3.0	0.1	12.2
1958	7.8	2.3	0.3	10.4

In addition to banking, the cooperatives perform a series of agricultural marketing functions. They act, for example, as agent for the Cyprus Grain Commission — purchasing excess wheat and barley from farmers and storing it for export or local consumption. They purchase surplus *zivania* (raw grape spirits) and raisins from the island's wine growers. They operate a pooling arrangement which ensures collection, processing, and export of the island's carob crop. In recent years the cooperatives have experimented with packing vegetables, mostly carrots and potatoes, for export.

There are also marketing cooperatives for a range of other agricultural products: citrus fruit cooperatives operate in Lapithos, Famagusta, and Karavas; all of the apricots in the area of Ayios Amvrosios near Kyrenia are sold through cooperatives; all of the island's cherries go to market through the Pedhoulas and Moutoullas associations; a vineyardists' cooperative known as S.O.D.A.P. manufactures wine, *ouzo,* alcohol, and brandy. In aggregate, about 50 per cent of the island's agricultural produce is marketed through direct or indirect assistance from the cooperatives.

Cooperative societies also offer purchasing facilities for a wide range of consumer and producer goods needed by Cyprus peasants. Simple household goods, DDT spray, fertilizers, seed of all kinds, and insecticides for crops are among the products sold regularly through village co-ops. Consumer groups grew from 16 in 1940 to more than 300 in 1958, as the volume of purchases expanded from $54,000 to $9 million in the same period.

The various parts of the cooperative movement on Cyprus are linked by the financial mechanism of two cooperative central banks. The banks operate essentially with the $5 million of deposits kept with them by the village and school savings societies. To protect themselves against bad crop years — as in 1956 and 1960 — the Greek and Turkish banks maintain a reserve fund of $1.2 million and an overdraft guarantee of about $2 million with Barclay's Bank and the Türkiye Ish Bankasi. This arrangement is backed by the government.

Along with its support to cooperatives, the Crown Colony government launched, after 1950, a broad-spectrum attack on the problems of agricultural production on Cyprus. This consisted of a machinery import scheme for pumps and tractors — today there are more than 3000 tractors working, one for every 350 acres of farmland — a well drilling program, and the development of an agricultural extension service. The program came partially from the British version of a "Point 4" philosophy and partially from the need to keep agricultural production on Cyprus from dropping, as military base construction drained laborers off the land to the towns.

Capital formation in agriculture grew in response to the expenditure on pumps and tractors — from 7 per cent of total investment in 1952 to about 10 per cent in recent years. While still low in respect to the percentage of the population dependent upon farming, the figures reflect an improvement brought about by the government's policies, prosperity and employment created by the bases, and the activity of the cooperatives.

The foregoing makes possible conflicting conclusions about Cyprus agriculture. On the side of optimism, British stewardship during the decade of the 1950's brought about impressive increases in cereal acreage and yield, in use of fertilizers, in land under irrigation, in reforestation, in development of commandaria wine production, in water utilization, and in the development of a cooperative movement of a truly outstanding character. Equally important, the colonial government installed fresh-water drinking installations in most villages, built schools in most as well, and linked the villages and district towns with a network of excellent, easily passable roads. The improvements wrought in the island's social overhead were substantial. These joined with employment on the base to impart fluidity and to retard formation of the hermetic seal which often isolates rural dwellers in the Middle East and which can so easily create a hopeless and apathetic peasantry.

One may also arrive at gloomy conclusions about Cyprus agriculture. In simple terms, despite recent improvements, Cyprus cannot feed itself. Each year it imports more than $25 million worth of agricultural products — cereals, oils, meat, dairy products, and eggs. Export of oranges, hard wheat (used for semolina flour making in Italy), carobs, wine, and potatoes partially pays for the imports. But the island, although an agricultural country, is incapable of sustaining itself at present consumption levels without food imports. Oranges and carobs are Cyprus' only really competitive exports, and these increasingly depend on a captive market in the United Kingdom or British Commonwealth.

A further basis for pessimism lies in the system of land tenure and utilization. Most experts agree that unless a cure for overfragmentation is found, it is hard to imagine further increases in investment and yield in three-quarters of the island's farmland. British rule did little to check the trend, and to date the government of the new Republic has likewise avoided a frontal attack on the problem.

The difference in income between rural and urban dwellers likewise presents a problem. The island's farm population, 50 per cent of the total, has a per capita income of about \$200 — less than half of the island's over-all per capita figure. Even after allowance for distorted figures (because of occasional town employment for some farmers) one can only reach the conclusion that the Cypriote farmer has little surplus for reinvestment in soil improvement. Under present technological limitations he cannot increase his output much further. Nor can he be part of a mass market for city factories. Despite his relative affluence on Middle Eastern standards, he still helps prove Ragnar Nurkse's thesis on the "vicious circle" of low productivity inhibiting increased purchasing power.

Rural Cyprus also, despite the fluidity and prosperity of the 1950's, suffers from substantial and chronic underemployment. As mentioned earlier, many peasants spend much of their working day traveling from plot to plot. Government economists offer estimates of underemployment ranging as high as 30 per cent of the rural labor force. Despite recent improvements, the organization of agricultural production is still very inefficient, and partially employed farmers make up a significant unused asset.

Further difficulty comes from price rises associated with

the expansion which Cyprus' economy underwent during the decade after 1950. Prices rose 65 per cent, including those of most items bought by farmers. Yet grain prices, subject to foreign competition, rose only slightly, and in some years dropped. The result was that Cyprus cereal production could not effectively compete with imported grain, and, under the circumstances, the government had no alternative but to buy wheat from peasants at 30 to 50 per cent above world prices. Citrus fruits, while more competitive, also depend on Commonwealth trading arrangements for their outlet.

Cyprus agriculture may be described, therefore, as a greatly improved yet still highly inadequate sustainer of 50 per cent of the island's population. Real advances have been made—particularly in cereal productivity, in cooperatives of various kinds, in chicken farming, and in citrus production. But the Cyprus farmer today still depends too heavily on the grain subsidy and on the safety valve of base jobs and emigration for his sons and daughters. Real viability for the island's farmers, most observers conclude, depends on a coupling of new technology (initially in improvements in water collection and usage) with reorganization of productive arrangements such as land tenure and usage. Problems of agriculture are central to the tasks facing the new Republic.

4

Industry

There was practically no industry in Cyprus prior to World War II. The copper mines, a few bottling plants, and a handful of construction enterprises made up the island's industrial sector. Upper-income Cypriotes ate, drank, traveled about in, and wore, products imported from England or the Continent. Even the lowest-income families clothed themselves mainly with British cotton and woolens. Copper and pyrites were the major exports, followed by small quantities of goat cheese and wine.

During and after World War II, Cyprus' industry expanded sharply — stimulated by the Middle East Supply Centre in Cairo, demand from troops and civilian base personnel, shortages of foreign manufactured goods, and high mineral prices. Between 1950 and 1958, mining and quarrying production grew 31 per cent, or about 3.4 per cent yearly; construction advanced 69 per cent, or 6.8 per cent yearly; production of gas, electricity, and water rose 800 per cent, or 31.6 per cent yearly; manufacturing grew 11.9 per cent, or 1.4 per cent yearly. By the end of the decade, industry was producing $50–$60 million yearly, about 25 per cent of Cyprus' national income. Of the total, mining accounted for an average of half, or 10 to 12 per cent of national income; manufacturing and construction shared the other half, and together accounted for another 10 to 12 per cent of national income.

A statistical breakdown of Cyprus' industries in 1954–55, a census year, is given in Table 10. The figures show that manufacturing enterprises of various kinds employed about half the total industrial labor force of just under 50,000, construction over 15,000, mining 6,000–7,000, and public utilities about 1,000. A look at the various sectors is illustrative of the island's industry.

In terms of contribution to national income, mining and quarrying are Cyprus' most important industry today. The mines have origins deep in antiquity. Cyprus was a major producer of the world's copper from the third millennium B.C. to Roman times, and indeed the word copper is related to the island's name. Most authorities agree that, except for desultory digging in Byzantine times, copper mining was largely neglected from late in the Roman era until the British occupation in 1878.

Copper mining revived in Cyprus through a stimulus given in the early twentieth century by an American mining engineer named Seeley Mudd. Possessed of an extracurricular interest in classical studies, Mudd made an unorthodox investment by employing an ancient historian to probe library sources on mining in Asia Minor, Persia, and the eastern Mediterranean in Hellenic and Roman times. The historian's findings pointed to the earlier existence of copper in what is now Turkey, in the Zagros Mountains in Iran, in the Sinai Desert of Egypt, and in Cyprus.

After exploratory drillings elsewhere in the Middle East,

TABLE 10

Size and output of industries in 1954

Industry	Number of establishments	Number of persons employed	Gross output[a] (dollars)	Net output[a] (dollars)
Mining and quarrying	355	6,716	27,106,996	23,704,570
Construction[b]	2,006	15,611	17,724,330	9,016,549
Manufacturing	11,328	26,293	45,003,873	13,145,472
Food	1,286	3,560	17,217,505	2,015,373
Beverages	258	1,361	5,582,830	1,888,320
Tobacco	7	377	4,793,197	629,465
Textiles and clothing	6,694	11,634	6,995,531	3,015,536
Wood products	830	2,101	2,540,700	1,107,725
Printing and publishing	86	734	1,099,476	624,375
Nonmetallic mineral products	305	1,606	1,743,834	985,082
Metal products	637	1,657	1,597,778	1,016,498
Transport equipment	421	1,438	1,059,330	785,518
Other	804	1,825	2,373,692	1,077,580
Public utilities	18	907	1,730,081	1,532,355
Total	13,707	49,527	91,565,280	47,398,946

Source: Government of Cyprus, *Census of Industry* (Nicosia, 1956).
[a] The output of cottage industries is not included in these figures.
[b] The figures for construction do not include the activities of H. M. Services, either direct or through large contractors.

Mudd chose Cyprus. He staked his claim in the foothills of the Troodos Mountains near the villages of Lefka and Skouriotissa. A somewhat skeptical Colonial Office, perhaps considering Mudd merely another eccentric from across the Atlantic — after all, the world's copper needs were already amply supplied by mines in America and Africa — made a lease concession which was notably generous. It called for the payment of a nominal royalty and, in the early years, a negligible income tax.

Mudd's company, the Cyprus Mines Corporation, went on over the forty years from 1905 to 1945 to develop the Mavrovouni Mine and other seams in its lease area. For part of the period the undertaking was probably more interesting to archaeologists than to the mine's owners. World copper prices were less than buoyant from 1900 to World War II, and the Mudd interests, selling ore and concentrates in Germany, ploughed a major part of their earnings back into improvement of the mines and facilities. Dividends were modest. The Cyprus Museum, meanwhile, accumulated a rich collection of artifacts and potsherds which helped prove, among other things, that the Mavrovouni Mine was indisputably one of the world's original sources of copper.

After World War II, production from the C.M.C. leases grew rapidly, spurred by soaring international metal and pyrites prices. Some of the mines' produce was exported after a single crushing, but most was treated before shipment in acid leaching and flotation plants. The resultant yields of cement copper, cupreous concentrates, and iron pyrites were moved to offshore vessels by lighter and sent to Germany for final sale and processing. Today Cyprus supplies about 1 per cent of the Free World's new copper.

Other metallic mining ventures began on Cyprus in the 1930's. These too expanded operations after the war. One was the Cyprus Sulphur and Copper Company, a British firm, which extracts cupreous pyrites from its mines at Kinousa and Limni. Another was the Hellenic Mining Company, originally Greek-owned, which extracts low-grade copper and iron ores from its shafts at Kalavasos, Kambia Sha, and Mitsero-

Agrokipia. A portion of the ore is treated in crushing and flotation plants at Vasilikos and Mitsero. Since independence, the Greek owners have turned over the assets of the Hellenic Mining Company to the Greek community of Cyprus. One other metallic mining venture operates in Cyprus, the Cyprus Chrome Company. Norwegian- and American-owned, the company's leases lie on the northwest slope of Mount Troodos, and chrome metal is extracted at the company's plants before export.

The only other minerals of export significance to Cyprus are asbestos and umber. The former is mined from serpentine rock by Cyprus Asbestos Mines, an Anglo-Danish firm, at Amiandos, near the top of Mount Troodos. After milling, graded asbestos fiber is either exported from Limassol or made into cement sheeting in the company's plants at Amiandos. Umber is mined in shallow pits near Larnaca. In the crude form or after pulverization, the umber powder is sold locally and exported throughout the eastern Mediterranean and Europe, the United States, and Australia to provide tinting for exterior building washes and paint dyes. In recent years both asbestos and umber have felt severe competition in export markets from synthetic substitutes made in western Europe.

Stone quarrying is also important to the domestic economy of Cyprus. Almost three hundred establishments operate, most of them one- or two-man operations, to provide materials for local building construction.

Coupled with their major role in terms of Cyprus' national income (and less important role in terms of employment), the mines account for more than half of Cyprus' foreign exchange earnings, pay three-quarters of the total income tax collected, account for one-quarter of the total ordinary revenue of government, and generate 50 to 60 per cent of the island's exports by value. Table 11 illustrates the export role of minerals.

The next important element in Cyprus' industry is construction. Between 1945 and 1958, the building and construction industry developed until it comprised more than 2,000 establishments, employing as many as 20,000 workers. In 1954, as Table 12 shows, 84 per cent of these establishments employed four workers or less — mainly carpenters and masons. The 300 firms employing from 5 to 1,000 or more workers employed men with a broader variety of skills and accounted for all of the major construction work on the island.

The tremendous expansion in construction on Cyprus came from pent-up purchasing power and urban housing shortages created by World War II, military base construction, the postwar government development program, which invested heavily in roads and public utilities, and the need for buildings of all kinds which accompanied the burgeoning of the island's six district towns.

Another element creating a rise in construction was the absence of alternative outlets for investment — plus preference of investors for real estate and buildings over holdings in industry and agriculture. This preference is partially built into the eastern Mediterranean culture pattern and is partially attributable to the flow of funds from England. Together these pulled Cypriote savings into housing in a growing wave. Occasional hints by the government that base construction and soldier quartering were destined to slacken only pushed investment in housing higher — as Cypriotes hastened to gain title to real estate as a cushion against possible currency devaluation should the boom really collapse.

The result of the postwar construction boom is illustrated dramatically by the 1958 figures on capital formation. In that year, 47 per cent of total investment in Cyprus, $22.5 million, went into construction. Of this, $13.5 million, more than half, went into dwellings, $3.6 million went into nonresidential

TABLE 11

Exports of minerals, 1953–1960

Mineral	Quantity (tons)							
	1953	1954	1955	1956	1957	1958	1959	1960
Asbestos	9,200	18,163	12,843	12,504	11,886	13,118	14,403	15,328
Cement copper	2,252	3,060	2,851	3,700	3,900	4,068	3,693	2,212
Chrome ore	7,277	9,867	8,570	5,826	5,070	11,840	12,176	14,020
Cupreous concentrates	81,085	93,610	77,765	119,211	139,192	115,125	123,519	115,784
Cupreous pyrites	129,915	125,370	139,230	171,032	226,334	228,821	307,026	248,931
Iron pyrites	565,183	687,954	753,640	821,727	762,501	819,835	659,370	815,412
Gypsum, calcined	7,420	6,877	3,747	3,023	1,256	2,722	1,538	2,144
Gypsum	94,720	91,663	89,998	25,424	41,687	27,067	52,304	107,560
Terra umbra	4,899	4,998	5,359	4,748	4,317	3,885	3,959	4,718
Other	616	764	1,001	1,464	1,219	1,275	1,360	922
Total	902,567	1,042,326	1,095,004	1,168,659	1,197,362	1,227,756	1,179,348	1,327,031
Total index[a]	95.4	108.9	102.3	125.6	134.3	131.0	134.6	133.6

Mineral	Value (thousands of dollars f.o.b.)							
	1953	1954	1955	1956	1957	1958	1959	1960
Asbestos	1,322	2,433	1,943	1,901	2,010	2,212	2,400	2,470
Cement copper	924	1,148	1,501	2,061	1,308	1,291	1,313	764
Chrome ore	333	392	272	188	185	420	384	412
Cupreous concentrates	7,862	10,321	11,724	18,542	10,892	8,450	11,172	12,130
Cupreous pyrites	3,343	2,811	3,349	5,048	5,068	4,178	5,592	4,502
Iron pyrites	7,568	9,346	9,999	10,766	9,461	8,599	5,295	6,426
Gypsum, calcined	106	728	36	28	11	34	17	22
Gypsum	232	162	165	42	78	84	148	302
Terra umbra	87	101	157	151	143	132	137	160
Other	14	22	34	39	34	36	31	22
Total	21,791	27,464	29,180	38,766	29,190	25,436	26,489	27,210
Total index[a]	142.8	175.7	191.2	254.0	191.3	166.7	173.6	178.3

[a] 1950 = 100. The quantity index is weighted by 1950 prices.

TABLE 12

Number of building and construction establishments of various sizes in 1954 (by number of employees)

	1	2–4	5–9	10–49	50–99	100–999	1,000 and over	Total
Number of establishments	1,218	477	132	144	13	20	2	2,006
Percentage of total	60.7	23.8	6.6	7.2	0.6	1.0	0.1	100.0

buildings (garages, industrial plants), and $5.5 million went into base construction, highways, and public utilities.

The third important category of industry in Cyprus is manufacturing. By 1954 more than 11,000 industrial enterprises were in operation. As shown in Table 13, most were one-man establishments, 94 per cent employed four persons or less, and only a handful were factories in the Western sense.

The island's food industries process local products entirely for the home market. Ninety per cent of them employ 4 persons or less. Included in the category are producers of prepared meats, dairy products, and preserved fruits and vegetables, grain millers, bakers, and confectioners. Within the group only two firms employ more than 50 workers, and one — a fruit canning plant — today employs more than 100.

Beverage manufacture follows much the same pattern. Over 250 establishments operate, most of them one-man businesses, and less than four of them employ as many as a hundred workers. In general, the same applies to the manufacture of tobacco, textiles, footwear, wood and furniture,

TABLE 13

Number of manufacturing establishments of various sizes in 1954
(by number of employees)

Manufacturing industry	1	2–4	5–9	10–49	50–99	100–999	1,000 and over	Total
Food (except beverages)	463	677	106	38	2	0	0	1,286
Beverages	167	57	15	12	4	3	0	258
Tobacco	0	0	0	4	2	1	0	7
Textiles	2	15	1	7	0	1	0	26
Footwear, apparel, and made-up textile goods	4,681	1,738	216	31	2	0	0	6,668
Wood and cork (except furniture)	16	61	16	9	0	0	0	102
Furniture and fixtures	300	365	58	5	0	0	0	728
Paper and paperboard	0	3	0	0	0	0	0	3
Printing and publishing	19	39	14	11	2	1	0	86
Leather and leather products	9	6	3	2	0	0	0	20
Rubber products	11	9	0	1	0	0	0	21
Chemicals	21	17	10	3	1	0	0	52
Nonmetallic mineral products	94	161	21	27	0	2	0	305
Metal products	247	197	30	10	0	0	0	484
Machinery (except electrical)	23	58	21	8	0	0	0	110
Electrical machinery	13	27	3	0	0	0	0	43
Transport equipment	134	207	62	16	2	0	0	421
Other	512	186	3	3	3	1	0	708
Total	6,712	3,823	579	187	18	9	0	11,328
Percentage of total	59.2	33.7	5.1	1.7	0.2	0.1	0.0	100.0

printing, leather, rubber products, nonmetallic mineral products, and the production of transport equipment.

Until 1952, the production of electric power in Cyprus was largely in the hands of about a dozen small producers, who produced from 2 to 3 million KWH yearly. In that year the Cyprus Electricity Authority, a public corporation, was created. The authority now operates a central generating plant at Dhekelia (which produced 193 million KWH in 1959), transmission lines over much of the island, and standby generators in several of the district towns. Many of the small producers still operate. In all, the electric power industry employs about 1,000 people, provides about 370 KWH per capita per year to Cypriotes — a high figure by eastern Mediterranean standards — and accounts for $2–$3 million of investment each year. Its phenomenal expansion was in response to Cyprus' economic growth and the spread of rural electrification.

After World War II, trade unionism grew rapidly in Cyprus. Between 1954 and 1958, for example (the period when most figures are available), trade unions grew from 130 to 284, and total membership expanded from about 26,000 to 56,000; the latter figure included almost all of the industrial labor force. By 1958, the Pan-Cyprian Federation of Labor claimed 31,723 members, the Cyprus Confederation of Free Trade Unions 12,800, the Cyprus Federation of Independent Trade Unions 2,036, the Cyprus Turkish Trade Unions Federation 1,137, the Civil Service Trade Unions 6,256, and other unions 2,538. Table 14 is illustrative.

TABLE 14

Number of trade unions and union members in 1958

Industrial activity	Unions	Members
Agriculture, fishing, and hunting	25	4,928
Mining and quarrying	32	2,302
Manufacturing	18	3,872
Construction	65	24,241
Electricity, gas, water, and sanitary services	3	794
Commerce	14	2,640
Transport, storage, and communications	25	3,683
Services	24	8,829
Other	78	5,253
Total	284	56,542

Trade unionism grew rapidly for several reasons. One was the constant encouragement given it after 1950 by officials and government decrees. Aided by Colonial Office policy directives — which in turn perhaps reflected earlier postwar Labour Government attitudes at home — as well as by the changing political outlook of the postwar breed of colonial Englishmen, the unions found a series of champions in government. Further explanation lies in the character of union leadership. Many Cypriote union organizers have been well-trained products of the left wing in Europe, and some have received postgraduate instruction in Moscow and Prague. They have, moreover, been of real assistance to the Cypriote worker — with well-run clinics, campaigns to keep wages advancing along with prices, and pressure on government. As in Israel, trade unions in Cyprus now claim the allegiance of practically the entire industrial labor force.

The sole pocket of resistance against the unions came from the copper mines. American and Greek owners withstood a series of strikes in 1953–54 and countered the unions' efforts until 1958, when low copper prices and increased mechanization (with resultant layoffs) joined to make mineworkers for the first time a receptive audience for organizers. Earlier, model working conditions in the mines, company clinics, fringe benefits and wage increases tied to cost of living indexes, implacable opposition from company managers, and isolated locations of the mines joined to keep unions ineffective in the mining industry. Since 1958 the mines have become partly unionized.

Another important element in Cyprus' industrial development — entrepreneurship — is harder to assess with accuracy. A few generalizations may be made: most really successful industrial enterprises in Cyprus have foreign management, process-control, or ownership somewhere in the arrangement — as in the copper mines, foreign-franchised bottling works such as Coca-Cola and Pepsi-Cola, or the larger fruit canning ventures; as elsewhere in the eastern Mediterranean, Armenians serve as a successful and creative industrial minority; until very recently most successful Cypriote-owned factories were run by owners of Greek extraction; those Cypriotes who became successful producing entrepreneurs were usually sons of trading families who had been educated abroad; most Cyprus factories betray the usual underdeveloped-area shortage of supervisory personnel and foremen in relation to workers — with resultant problems of quality control and output.

Yet to say more about Cypriotes' qualities as entrepreneurs is difficult. Too many forces joined, in the period of post–World War II expansion, to obscure the role of the enterpriser in the Schumpeterian sense. Sterling area currency controls, for example, unquestionably hobbled the more adventuresome businessmen and kept them from the East-West entrepôt trade; at no time during the period in question did Cyprus have adequate port facilities or free zone warehouses; post-war rises in money supply and prices on the island ruled Cyprus goods off world markets — except those guaranteed by Commonwealth trading arrangements; the domestic market in Cyprus was too narrow to permit, except for a few industries, economies of scale and really efficient production. Accurate measurement of the actual contribution of the entrepreneur to economic growth in Cyprus remains a speculative task.

Less characterized by speculation are a series of patterns which accompany the foregoing analysis of industry in Cyprus. The first of these relates to productivity. As shown in Table 15, the only industries whose productivity per man-year by 1954 had even approached that of middle-income nations were mining, beverage and tobacco making, and public utilities.

TABLE 15

Net annual output per industrial employee, 1950 and 1954 (dollars)

Industry	1950	1954
Food manufacturing	247	202
Beverage manufacturing	552	490
Tobacco manufacturing	446	590
Textile and clothing manufacturing	—	92
Wood manufacturing	98	188
Printing and publishing	328	304
Nonmetallic mineral products	179	218
Metal products	—	220
Transport equipment	168	196
Other manufactures	—	210
Mining and quarrying	764	1,261
Construction	148	206
Public utilities	379	630
Average for manufacturing[a]	—	178
Average for all industries	—	343

Source: Government of Cyprus, Census of Industry (Nicosia, 1956).

[a] All industries except mining, construction, and public utilities.

Mining was producing a respectable $1,261 per man-year by then, and it was the only industry to show a sharp rise in productivity between 1950 and 1954. Meanwhile, the island's over-all average for manufacturing (that is, for all industry except mining, construction, and public utilities) was only $178 per man-year. Even including the three most productive ventures, the islandwide average for all industries was only $343. On man-year standards, Cyprus industry is *highly* unproductive.

Costs of production reflect the combination of the island's increasing money supply and inflation, the built-in cost-push resulting from its well organized trade unions, and its low productivity per worker. While no definitive studies have been made, sample assessments in 1958 and 1959 by Crown Colony statisticians concluded that costs of production of selected food products and textiles were 40 per cent higher than those in Holland. A sizable export trade is thus, under present circumstances, out of the question.

A corollary to the above has been the demonstrated inability of Cyprus' manufacturing to hold its own, in percentage terms, as generator of the island's gross domestic product. As indicated in Table 16, manufacturing sank from generating 15 per cent of the gross domestic product in 1950 to providing only 11 per cent by 1959. While there are no absolute norms of judgment as to desirable structures of national income,

TABLE 16

Contribution of manufacturing industries to gross domestic product, 1950–1960

Year	Contribution at current prices (millions of dollars)	Percentage of gross domestic product
1950	16.5	15.2
1951	17.9	13.9
1952	18.2	11.9
1953	19.6	11.7
1954	19.0	10.8
1955	21.6	11.5
1956	23.2	10.3
1957	24.1	10.2
1958	22.4	10.0
1959	23.5	11.0
1960	24.1	11.5

recent comparative assessments would indicate that, on international standards, Cyprus' income levels and size should support manufacturing at at least the 1950 level — 15 per cent of the gross domestic product.* Yet the trend of the past decade was downward.

The figures on investment in manufacturing enterprises in Cyprus accent the trend described. Investment in manufacturing rose from about $7.5 million in 1954 to about $12 million in 1956. After that it dropped off to about $9 million. Compared to the island-wide investment figure of close to $50 million (much of it for construction), investment in manufacturing was small. When one compares it, moreover, to the figures in Tables 16 and 17, one can only conclude that the investment had relatively little over-all effect.

Another feature of manufacturing industry in Cyprus is the lack of interdependence between enterprises. As is shown graphically in the Appendix, very little buying and selling of products between firms goes on. With few exceptions, firms either import their requirements (sugar, concentrates, and machinery in the case of bottling plants, textiles and yarn in the case of clothing establishments) or buy them from the island's agricultural producers. Some interdependence between agriculture and industry exists. But there is little within the industrial sector. And the low productivity of most industrial workers does not afford them sufficient purchasing power to buy large quantities of goods from other factories. The frontal attack on the economic frontier envisaged by Ragnar Nurkse (in which the goods from one man's factory are bought by workers in another man's factory, and vice versa) has simply not begun.

A related problem, suggested in Chapter 3, is that of the

* See Hollis Chenery, "Patterns of Industrial Growth," *American Economic Review*, September 1960.

TABLE 17

Index of industrial origin of gross domestic product at current factor cost, 1950–1960

	1950	1951	1952	1953	1954	1955	1956	1957	1958	1959	1960
Agriculture, forestry, fishing, and hunting	100.0	117.0	147.2	184.0	165.1	154.7	185.8	171.7	168.9	158.5	144.3
Manufacturing	100.0	108.5	110.2	118.6	115.3	130.5	140.7	145.8	135.6	142.4	145.8
Mining and quarrying	100.0	145.8	189.6	143.7	177.1	191.7	237.5	191.7	166.7	175.0	181.3
Construction	100.0	130.8	176.9	223.1	300.0	307.7	330.8	338.5	307.7	246.2	230.8
Electricity, gas, and water	100.0	100.0	100.0	150.0	300.0	400.0	600.0	800.0	900.0	1,000.0	1,150.0
Transportation, storage, and communication	100.0	140.0	173.3	206.7	246.7	280.0	333.3	346.7	320.0	320.0	306.7
Wholesale and retail trade	100.0	109.3	120.9	132.6	151.2	179.1	209.3	239.5	181.4	186.0	181.4
Banking, insurance, and real estate	100.0	116.7	133.3	133.3	150.0	200.0	266.7	266.7	283.3	283.3	283.3
Ownership of dwellings	100.0	104.2	112.5	133.3	150.0	166.7	195.8	220.8	237.5	241.7	241.7
Public administration and defense	100.0	108.8	117.6	132.4	147.1	176.5	288.2	423.5	458.8	352.9	338.2
Services	100.0	127.0	148.6	164.9	164.9	154.1	156.8	145.9	135.1	148.6	148.6
Gross domestic product at factor cost	100.0	119.1	140.8	155.0	163.0	172.9	208.8	217.6	207.5	197.9	193.3
Net national income	100.0	119.7	142.3	156.3	163.4	173.0	194.9	211.0	204.8	196.1	184.2

absence of a really reformed agriculture giving sustenance to dynamic industry. With a per capita income half the island's average, the Cypriote cereal grower can neither save enough to invest in increased output from his land nor buy much from the island's factories. So the factories live mainly from markets in urban Cyprus, which in turn are sustained by troops quartered on the island.

In summary, the foreign-owned mining companies are the most dynamic industry on Cyprus. The most vigorous domestic industry is construction, and most of the funds ploughed into the island since World War II have gone into buildings of various kinds; too few, unfortunately, have been invested in industrial buildings. Manufacturing is decidedly the weakest part of the island's industry. The role of manufacturing as generator of national income dropped during the 1950's; recent new investment, while small, has gone largely to create new (and mostly unused) plant capacity rather than to generate more production or jobs; no manufactured product from Cyprus has established itself as competitively superior in world markets; costs of production are high and productivity is low. Like agriculture, industry in Cyprus is in need of marked improvement if self-sustaining economic growth is to begin.

5

Trade, Banking, and Government

As shown earlier, farming, mining, manufacturing, and construction together produce about half Cyprus' national income and employ about three-quarters of the labor force. The remaining 50 per cent of the national income, and employment for the final quarter of those gainfully employed, are accounted for by an aggregate of occupations in trade, banking, real estate, public administration and defense, and services of various kinds.

The Crown Colony conducted its first census of distribution in 1957, and concluded that at the time there were 477 wholesale and 6,819 retail trading establishments on the island. The wholesale firms dealt mainly in foods, textiles or clothing, and general merchandise or served as commission agents. Just over 3,000 persons made a living from wholesale trade. Retail trade, on the other hand, employed almost 10,000 people, mostly in one-man businesses. Retail stores sold the usual range of foods, clothing, and miscellaneous household needs. About half the trading firms are located in the island's six district towns, and the others spread through the network of Mesaoria and mountain villages.

As in nearby Arab countries, wholesale and retail trade on Cyprus are often carried on in the same establishments. But there is considerable specialization in products, and the dealer's showroom piled high with crates of Scotch whiskey and cologne water alongside European automobiles is rarer in Cyprus than elsewhere in the eastern Mediterranean. These circumstances seem to indicate more knowledge by dealers of the products they sell, and also discourages the time-consuming bargaining which distinguishes trade at all levels throughout the Levant.

Much of trade on Cyprus has its origin directly in imports. From 1953 to 1959, the value of imports almost doubled, from just under $60 million to $115 million (though it dropped slightly in the following year). By 1959, producers' goods (industrial raw materials, machinery, and so forth) had come to comprise about 47 per cent of the total, consumers' goods (food, tobacco, beverages, and the rest) another 41 per cent, and fuel and lubricants 11 per cent. In 1953, 60 per cent of imports came from sterling area countries and most of the remaining 40 per cent from OEEC countries. Six years later, because of Cypriotes' boycott of British goods and liberalization of trade with Europe, percentages shifted to 48 per cent from the sterling area and 52 per cent from elsewhere. Dollar area imports during the same period underwent a decline from 5 per cent in 1953 to just under 4 per cent in 1959.

The commodities imported over the seven-year period 1953–1960, as shown in Table 18, showed a general increase — imports of many items doubled in value. Beverages and tobacco and miscellaneous manufactured articles (such as electric appliances), however, showed the standard under-developed-area pattern of most rapid increase. These grew

TABLE 18

Value (c.i.f.) of imports, 1953–1960 (millions of dollars)

Import[a]	1953	1954	1955	1956	1957	1958	1959	1960
Food	8.7	8.1	11.2	16.2	16.2	15.7	16.8	20.2
Beverages and tobacco	1.1	1.1	2.0	3.9	4.8	3.9	5.0	4.5
Crude materials	2.5	2.8	3.1	4.2	4.2	3.4	3.6	3.4
Mineral fuels	5.6	5.9	7.0	10.9	13.2	11.5	10.6	10.4
Animal and vegetable oils	1.1	1.4	1.4	2.0	1.4	1.7	2.0	2.2
Chemicals	3.9	4.2	5.0	7.3	8.7	8.1	9.2	9.2
Manufactured goods	17.9	19.6	23.5	26.9	30.8	23.5	28.6	24.6
Machinery and transport equipment	11.8	15.4	22.4	25.8	29.7	20.4	21.8	19.6
Miscellaneous manufactured articles	5.9	6.7	8.7	11.5	16.2	12.9	15.7	12.9
Miscellaneous transactions and commodities, n.e.s.	0.8	0.8	0.8	0.8	1.4	1.4	1.7	2.5
Total	59.3	66.0	85.1	109.5	126.6	102.5	115.0	109.5

[a] Standard international trade classification sections.

more than four times for the first two and more than double for the third. Producers' goods of various kinds showed a more modest increase. While the over-all rise stemmed partly from demand created by British troops and by rising world prices of manufactured goods, the growth came mainly from higher incomes and increased purchasing power enjoyed by Cypriotes.

In contrast to imports, exports from Cyprus showed a very modest increase in value after 1953 — growing from just over $43 million to just under $54 million by 1960. Table 19 is illustrative. It makes clear that the big increases in export value over the years were made by mineral shipments. These reached a peak in the prosperous years 1955–1956 and then dropped back as world metal prices slipped in 1957 and 1958.

TABLE 19

Value (f.o.b.) of exports, 1953–1960 (millions of dollars)

Export[a]	1953	1954	1955	1956	1957	1958	1959	1960
Food	14.0	13.7	14.6	14.8	14.3	14.0	15.7	15.1
Beverages and tobacco	2.0	1.7	2.2	2.2	2.5	3.6	2.5	2.5
Crude materials	23.8	28.6	31.1	40.9	31.1	26.9	28.7	29.7
Mineral fuels	0.3	0.8	0.6	0.8	1.1	0.3	0.3	0.3
Animal and vegetable oils	0.0	}	0.3	0.3	0.3	0.3	0.3	0.0
		0.3						
Chemicals	0.3	0.0	0.0	0.3	0.0	0.0	0.0	0.0
Manufactured goods	0.3	0.3	0.8	0.3	0.6	0.3	0.6	0.6
Machinery and transport equipment	0.6	0.8	0.8	1.4	1.4	2.2	3.1	3.1
Miscellaneous manufactured articles	1.1	0.8	0.6	0.6	0.6	0.6	0.8	0.8
Miscellaneous transactions and commodities, n.e.s.	0.8	0.6	0.8	1.1	1.1	1.1	1.4	1.7
Total	43.2	47.6	51.8	62.7	53.0	49.3	53.4	53.8

[a] Standard international trade classification sections.

Wine and spirits exports also went up, owing to sales abroad of increasing quantities of brandy and bulk wines, particularly in years of poor vintage in Europe. Food exports held fairly steady, and were made up of hard semolina wheat, carobs, and citrus fruits.

Over the years under scrutiny, the proportional regional distribution of exports (in terms of value) underwent little change. Just over a third of Cyprus' exports (mainly citrus fruits, carobs, potatoes, and wine and brandy) went to the United Kingdom or elsewhere in the sterling area. Close to two thirds, the output of the island's mines, went mostly to Germany and other European countries.

Cyprus' terms of trade (its ratio of import prices to export prices) since 1950 have confounded the Cassandras who made dire predictions for the underdeveloped areas on the subject during the 1950's. Instead of suffering worsening ratios, caused by rising costs of imports and dropping prices of exports, the island managed some improvement in its terms of trade. Table 20 is illustrative. The gains were made despite a sharp

TABLE 20

Ratio of import costs to export prices, 1951–1960

Year	Ratio including mineral prices[a]	Ratio excluding mineral prices[a]
1951	81.4	100.6
1952	76.0	101.0
1953	72.9	95.2
1954	66.7	89.8
1955	65.2	89.9
1956	59.2	87.7
1957	75.0	95.5
1958	74.8	82.1
1959	76.3	86.1
1960	75.3	82.5

[a] The period 1946–1950 = 100.

domestic price rise, and came largely from even greater price rises abroad for citrus fruits, carobs, and copper and iron concentrates. The improvement also came from increased efficiency in the mines and from the fact that the island's citrus and carob exports were not subject to price increases created by higher labor costs.

Cyprus' trade balances reflect the increase in total value of imports over exports after 1950. In 1960, just under $54 million worth of exports went abroad, and just under $110 million of imports came onto the island. The actual magnitude of the adverse balance was about $56 million — an amount equal to $97 per Cypriote — and came to almost 20 per cent of the island's total gross national product. On international standards, Cyprus' dependence on imports is high indeed.

Yet for Cyprus, as for nearby Lebanon and Israel, the adverse trade balances of the 1950's did not lead to equal unbalance in over-all payments. As Table 21 shows, the trade deficit was fully covered by various invisible items on current account and by capital inflow. While Lebanon balanced its import deficits with invisible earnings in international trade and finance (plus emigrant remittances), and Israel covered its staggering import deficit with German reparations, gifts by international Jewry, foreign aid, and additions to foreign debt, Cyprus relied mainly on transfers from the United Kingdom Treasury. These varied between $40 million and $60 million in the later years of the decade, and went mostly for troop expenditures and local purchases of various kinds. In aggregate, the combination of base expenditures, emigrant remittances (which have averaged over $8 million yearly in recent years), and earnings from tourism covered Cyprus' import deficits.

Remittances from emigrants — which now average about $17 yearly for each Cypriote at home — are attributable to the skill shown by Cypriotes in commercial and industrial enterprises in Africa, England, and Latin America, and to their retention of loyalties to families and villages on the island. Like nearby Lebanese, many of the three to four thousand Cypriotes who emigrate each year return to the island for holidays, send funds home, and return with their life savings upon retirement.

Tourism is also closely related to trade in Cyprus. Visitors from abroad bring funds, purchase items brought in or made on the island, and create economic activity generally.

Prior to 1950, Cyprus appealed as a tourist center chiefly to those resident in nearby Eastern Shore countries, for whom Mount Troodos offered a cool retreat. American and European tourists were busy rediscovering Italy, the Tyrol, the Louvre, and the Parthenon, and only an occasional stray traveler or Philhellene from the West came to Cyprus. After 1950, prosperity in America and western Europe pushed growing numbers of tourists eastward, and Cyprus began to get its share. More than 30,000 tourists visited the island in 1954, and they

TABLE 21

Balance of Payments, 1952–1960 (millions of dollars)

	1952		1953		1954		1955	
	R	P	R	P	R	P	R	P
Goods and Services								
Merchandise (adjusted)[a]	50.05	50.43	42.53	50.79	46.68	57.18	51.44	73.56
Nonmonetary gold	[b]	−0.03	[b]	[b]	[b]	[b]	[b]	[b]
Foreign travel	3.36	2.60	4.23	2.72	5.46	2.60	4.90	2.80
Transport and insurance	0.90	8.04	1.12	9.07	2.38	10.50	2.69	12.38
Investment income	0.45	11.26	2.24	10.25	0.81	8.96	2.07	12.24
Government transactions	11.65	0.64	12.12	0.08	18.84	.08	28.28	0.08
Miscellaneous	0.42	0.90	0.81	1.32	0.50	2.69	0.70	2 80
Total	66.83	73.84	63.05	74.23	74.67	82.01	90.08	103.86
Donations								
Private	4.03	2.80	3.95	1.82	6.38	2.02	7.00	2.13
Official	0.08	[b]	1.29	[b]	1.71	[b]	0.39	[b]
Total	4.11	2.80	5.24	1.82	8.09	2.02	7.39	2.13
Capital								
Private	0.00	0.00	0.00	0.00	4.26	1.34	4.42	0.72
Official and banking institutions	6.63	11.03	2.35	4.81	2.58	6.41	17.98	15.15
Total	6.63	11.03	2.35	4.81	6.84	7.75	22.40	15.87
Errors and omissions	10.11	0.00	10.22	0.00	2.18	0.00	1.99	0.00
Grand total	87.67	87.67	80.86	80.86	91.78	91.78	121.86	121.86

[a] "Merchandise (adjusted)" differs from trade account figures because imports are adjusted by deducting freight and insurance charges and exports by deducting ships' stores. These items

left an estimated $10 million in the hands of merchants, transport operators, and hotel-keepers.

Between 1954 and 1958 the number of tourists dropped steadily to less than 10,000, costing Cyprus' economy an estimated $6 million yearly. Tourists stayed away during the political disturbances not so much because of real danger — EOKA's gunmen with few exceptions chose fellow Cypriotes or resident Britons as victims — but rather for reasons of inconvenience. The roadblocks and curfews joined with fear

TABLE 21

(Continued)

	1956		1957		1958		1959		1960	
	R	P	R	P	R	P	R	P	R	P
Goods and Services										
Merchandise (adjusted)[a]	62.19	95.82	53.76	109.96	50.82	88.96	54.21	102.42	55.55	93.77
Nonmonetary gold	b	b	b	b	b	b	b	b	b	b
Foreign travel	3.44	3.02	3.14	4.23	4.17	5.12	5.54	7.44	6.72	8.29
Transport and insurance	3.70	15.71	4.76	19.88	5.18	17.53	5.32	18.65	5.13	18.45
Investment income	2.69	26.35	1.18	17.58	2.13	13.66	1.62	16.27	2.66	18.53
Government transactions	56.87	0.11	45.36	0.62	44.74	0.87	39.20	0.45	49.84	0.39
Miscellaneous	2.13	2.80	2.80	2.80	2.80	2.80	2.80	2.80	2.80	2.80
Total	131.02	143.81	111.00	155.07	109.84	128.94	108.69	148.03	122.70	142.23
Donations										
Private	8.68	1.26	10.02	0.87	8.40	1.15	8.40	0.90	6.02	0.56
Official	2.10	b	13.44	b	18.98	b	16.44	b	11.70	b
Total	10.78	1.26	23.46	0.87	27.38	1.15	24.84	0.90	17.72	0.56
Capital										
Private	5.18	5.57	2.30	1.43	0.98	1.82	2.72	16.13	4.65	5.49
Official and banking institutions	11.84	15.88	12.77	2.60	5.55	10.72	26.43	2.80	2.74	0.56
Total	17.02	21.45	15.07	4.03	6.53	12.54	29.15	18.93	7.39	6.05
Errors and omissions	7.70	0.00	10.44	0.00	0.00	1.12	5.18	0.00	1.03	0.00
Grand total	166.52	166.52	159.97	159.97	143.75	143.75	167.86	167.86	148.84	148.84

are included in "Transport and insurance."

[b] Negligible amount.

of an act of idiocy by an adolescent gunman to discourage all but the most hardened holiday travelers.

Political troubles likewise discouraged expansion of hotel facilities during the decade of the 1950's. The island now has about a hundred hotels, offering accommodations in just over 2,000 rooms. Of these, no more than twelve hotels, with about 750 rooms, may be labeled as attractive to the European or American tourist. Hotel space is inadequate in the mountains, and the pleasant beaches on the north coast are, except for two hotels in Kyrenia, devoid of accommodations for tourists. The island possesses facilities with which to earn about $10 million yearly from tourists — but little more.

Banking in Cyprus is well developed, on standards of lower-income areas of the world. The Ottoman Bank, now an Anglo-French firm, first began on the island in 1854. Since then, eight other banks have opened, and together the banks operate more than thirty branches and employ almost 900 people. The island's largest financial establishment, the Bank of Cyprus, is purely a Cypriote undertaking. It began in 1899, and during the 1940's and 1950's expanded dramatically by mergers with a series of small Cypriote-owned banks in the district towns. It even opened a branch in London in 1955 — at the onset of the troubles between Britain and the island over Enosis.

The presence of branch banks in the island's towns and villages joined with the government's publicity campaigns to encourage bank savings throughout the island after World War II. Restrictions on movements of gold to and from the island also discouraged the hoarding common in nearby countries. So too did expansion of the money supply. In the seven-year period 1950–1957, the total of currency in circulation and bank deposits rose from just under $45 million to just under $126 million.

By early 1959 combined bank deposits reached $105 million and the statement of liabilities and assets for the banks on Cyprus looked as shown in Table 22. Of the $105 million in

TABLE 22

Cyprus banks' consolidated balance sheet, 1958–1960
(millions of dollars)

	1958	1959	1960
Liabilities			
Deposits	105.3	105.7	108.5
Balances due to other local banks	5.7	3.9	7.9
Balances due to banks abroad	3.1	6.5	9.5
Other liabilities	15.9	21.8	22.9
Total	130.0	137.9	148.8
Assets			
Cash	3.5	3.1	3.3
Balances due from other local banks	9.7	5.9	8.3
Balances due from banks abroad	19.1	8.1	6.4
Loans and advances	62.0	79.4	90.8
Local bills discounted	5.0	7.5	6.0
Local investments	1.1	1.3	3.3
Foreign investments	14.9	10.6	14.5
Other assets	14.7	22.0	16.2
Total	130.0	137.9	148.8

deposits, $35 million were savings bank deposits, $4 million were weekly deposits, $46.7 million were sight-and-demand deposits, and $23.2 million were fixed deposits. Within the various categories of deposits, about $87 million represented private funds and about $18 million were government monies of various kinds.

Bank loans and advances in early 1959 totaled $62 million — about 60 per cent of total deposits. These loans went about

34 per cent to finance wholesale and retail trade and 23 per cent to finance local industries and manufactures. Transport, government, and personal loans of various kinds claimed another 17 per cent of the loans and advances. Meanwhile the island's main pillars of sustenance, farming and mining, acquired only 17 per cent of the total credit.

Cyprus banks traditionally have issued loans following their own concepts of liquidity and collateral. While the island remained a Crown colony, there was no bank of issue. Central bank control of credit through bank rates (and the other measures of the Bank of England and the Federal Reserve in the United States) never evolved before independence. After 1955 the government, fearful of the role played by bank credit in fueling Cyprus' inflation, decreed that the island's banks should in future lend no more than 30 per cent of new deposits. There is little evidence that bankers complied; most continued, for the remainder of the decade, to lend nearer to 70 per cent of deposits, old and new.

The Cyprus currency, employing the decimal system of 1000 mils to the pound, is tied to sterling. It is now administered by a civil servant, the Commissioner of Currency, who conducts currency operations through the Ottoman Bank. In mid-1960, notes and coins worth about $25 million circulated, and the currency issue was backed, in the amount of about 108 per cent of the total note issue, by a currency fund in London. The latter is made up of about half United Kingdom securities of various kinds, a third Cyprus government bonds, and the remainder sterling deposits. The backing for the Cyprus pound was built up from budget surpluses over the years of British colonial rule.

The link to sterling, the interchangeability between it and sterling, and the strong backing of the note issue joined during the 1950's to prevent major fluctuations in the value of the Cyprus pound. Despite inflation and the emergency, the pound varied little in international markets.

In contrast to its role in banking, government in other areas plays a most important role in Cyprus' economy. Employment figures are indicative. The 37 government departments — ranging from Agriculture and Antiquities to Treasury and Water Development — employed in early 1959 a total of 5,270 workers. An additional 5,800 men and women worked in the Cyprus police and prison force, and as elementary and secondary school teachers. A total of just over 11,000 made up the government work force at the end of the 1950's.

Government of Cyprus revenues had grown, by 1960, to a total of over $61 million. All but a negligible part came from three sources: expenditure taxes of various kinds (import duties, liquor and tobacco taxes, levies on gasoline, and so forth) made up over $26 million; income taxes provided over $12 million; and external grants from the United Kingdom treasury, mostly designed to cover public works expenditures useful to the bases, made up almost another $12 million. The government budget almost tripled between 1952 and 1960 (as shown in Table 23).

During the decade of the 1950's government income from expenditure taxes held quite steady and provided about 50 per cent of total income in most years. Income taxes dwindled from 30 per cent to less than 20 per cent of total revenues; external grants as part of government revenue rose sharply.

Expenditures by government grew proportionately during the decade, from just under $20 million in 1950 to about $71 million in 1958. Of the totals, administrative services (cost of government) accounted for just over a third, social services (education, hospitals, and so forth) just under a third, and resource development (mainly public works, agriculture, and forestry) and miscellaneous items another third. During 1958,

TABLE 23

Government revenue, 1953–1960 (thousands of dollars)

Sources	1952	1953	1954	1955	1956	1957	1958	1959	1960
Taxes on expenditure	11,766	12,914	14,470	18,066	19,628	25,511	22,753	27,342	26,466
Taxes on income	7,949	9,414	7,888	9,075	12,510	15,686	12,466	10,077	12,079
Taxes on capital	622	823	882	935	946	451	414	490	563
Rents, royalties, and interest	692	893	1,028	1,056	3,948	2,307	2,383	2,971	2,909
External grants	0	0	1,400	0	2,100	13,440	18,992	16,428	11,701
Other	2,209	2,775	4,018	3,335	3,102	5,247	4,105	7,252	7,638
Total	23,238	26,819	29,686	32,467	42,234	62,642	61,113	64,560	61,356

the gap between income and expenditures was provided by transfers from the United Kingdom treasury. By the end of the decade, government expenditures were running to more than 30 per cent of national income.

The foregoing permits several conclusions which fill in further the outline of Cyprus' economy taking shape in earlier chapters. The first of these is that the 25 per cent of Cypriotes engaged in trade, banking, and government, who generate 50 per cent of the island's national income, are more productive than those in industry and agriculture. In the absence of studies, and because of the different criteria of productivity, exact comparisons are impossible. But the island's trading firms, banks, and government bureaus contrast sharply in efficiency with its farms and most of its industrial establishments.

Next, the export–import statistics make clear that during the 1950's only a small amount of import-substituting industry developed. The big increases in imports were in consumer goods, and Cyprus factories apparently gained only a small part of the market. The poor performance may in part be attributable to failure of the island's merchants — historically the source of its industrial entrepreneurship — to develop opportunities to produce import substitutes.

Next, the recent trading position of Cyprus accents the problems facing the new Republic with regard to future commercial policy. Its current Commonwealth status permits Cyprus to participate in trade under preferential tariff arrangements with other Commonwealth partners. In recent years, there is little doubt that Cyprus' citrus fruits, carobs, potatoes, and wines — 37 per cent of its exports — were salable in Commonwealth countries largely because of tariff cuts averaging over 14 per cent of value. Yet Cyprus in turn had to reciprocate with tariff reductions of its own. During 1958, in aggregate, Cyprus gained concessions worth about

$2.5 million, while it granted concessions worth over $3 million. Membership in the Commonwealth bloc, therefore, probably guaranteed a market for Cyprus' relatively expensive — and noncompetitive — agricultural products. But it also protected the Cyprus market for the likewise relatively expensive (compared to products from Germany, Italy, and Japan, for example) exports of Commonwealth nations.

Further, Cyprus faces problems with regard to its exports to Europe. Another 50 per cent of Cyprus' exports, in value, its minerals, go to countries now in the O.E.E.C. and prospectively members of the Common Market or the European Free Trading Association — the "Six" and the "Seven." Almost 90 per cent of the island's exports, in short, have been subject to some form of bloc arrangement. With efficient mineral producers and inefficient agricultural producers, the new government faces important and complicated decisions with regard to continuing in bloc trading, or shifting to bilateral or multilateral arrangements.

The foregoing likewise accents the relative lack in Cyprus of bank funds for long-term loans to industry. Cyprus banks historically have lent the bulk of their funds to merchants to finance short-term commercial transactions such as consumer imports, or to builders of town apartment houses. Cyprus has no securities market, and its industrial firms are excessively dependent on family funds or on renewable short-term advances (often at very high interest rates) from banks.

Yet another problem relates to the currency of the new Republic of Cyprus. Broadly speaking, the government faces two alternatives when its bank of issue, called for in the Constitution, begins operations. Having elected a ten year term in the sterling area, it can continue to regulate its currency supply, as the Commissioner of Currency has done in recent years, according to the supply and demand for British pounds in trading. Or it can, while still retaining sterling area membership, adopt a more flexible currency system, more adjustable to internal needs of the economy than to the balance of payments. Many observers feel that the second alternative will prevail — because of the need for access to the London money market, need for Commonwealth outlets for agricultural exports, political considerations associated with the bases, and the hope that more flexibility will encourage Cypriote bankers and merchants to try their luck in the East-West entrepôt trade.

Finally, the foregoing has emphasized the enormous role played by government in the economy of Cyprus. Government expenditures for the decade of the 1950's averaged well over 25 per cent of national income. Certainly well over 25 per cent of national income was directly or indirectly due to demand created by military transfers of various kinds. Government investments in infrastructure — the power grid, highways, and schools — were large. Much of private investment was calculated to satisfy demand created by government expenditures. Even on the standards of oil-producing countries in the Middle East and of Israel — which together show extreme reliance on government in economic life — the part played by government in Cyprus is huge.

6

Recent Economic Performance and the Future

Studies by the colonial government (and since September 1960 by the Finance Ministry of the new Republic of Cyprus) have concluded that the island's national income ceased its steep ascent sometime during late 1957. Climaxing twelve postwar years of extremely rapid rise, drops of about 3 per cent occurred during 1958, 4.3 per cent during 1959, and 6 per cent during 1960 — a total cut of 12.7 per cent since 1957. The 1958–1959 decline corresponded almost exactly with reduced United Kingdom military expenditures. The lower national income was accompanied by slight cuts in cost of living increases and a definite check in the dramatic price instability which had accompanied Cyprus' economic expansion for a decade.

On a sectoral basis, large drops in income occurred in agriculture, chiefly because of low rainfall throughout the eastern Mediterranean during the years 1957–1959. This led to sharp cuts in cereal yields and to lower net incomes from potato sales. There were also cuts in income arising from government, owing to lower base investment by Britain during the period of uncertainty leading to political independence. Income from services too reflected the downward trend. Industrial income alone rose slightly during 1959, chiefly because of increased sales of electricity and higher earnings from mineral exports. Yet despite the small improvement in industry, the net drop in income during 1959 totaled about $8,680,000, and in 1960, $11,760,000.

Investment too dropped sharply after 1957. From a high in that year of about 25 per cent of national income, new investment went on during 1958 and 1959 at just under 17 per cent of the reduced national income. While the percentage figure was still high by underdeveloped-area standards, the composition remained lopsided, as it had for a decade. Investment in housing construction still predominated, the main difference being that Cypriotes no longer built luxury flats in Nicosia but built instead closer to the British bases near Larnaca and Limassol.

The years 1958–1959 also marked a period of a rise in consumption expenditures by Cypriotes. Purchases went mainly for automobiles and other consumer durables. One explanation for this is that those with liquid savings were pessimistic about the Republic's economic future and preferred ownership of goods to bank balances. Many Cypriote civil servants also rushed to make purchases while Her Majesty's Government still stood ready to guarantee the loans — perhaps in expectation of more conservative policies from the government of the new Republic. Others applied for loans while the Bank of Cyprus was still in a mood, as it had been since 1954, to practice liberal lending policies.

The drops in investment and national income after 1957

were also accompanied by rises in unemployment. From full employment in 1957, the lists of registered unemployed grew to over 6,000 by the summer of 1960 and to 7,500 by early 1961. Yet to assess unemployment exactly remains difficult. Undoubtedly many of the jobless returned to their villages and were partially reabsorbed into agriculture. Others, more urban, refrained from registering on the assumption that their old employers would call them back when work commenced. Trade unionists estimated that unemployment in mid-1960 was nearer to 15,000.

Another feature of the years 1957–1960 was a transfer of capital from Cyprus into sterling accounts in London and into other currencies elsewhere, mostly in Switzerland. Some of this went on through the smuggling of banknotes and exchange of these in Beirut and Zurich. Other funds left via the technique, common to merchants in currency-controlled economies, of undervaluing exports and overvaluing imports. The island's bankers and financial officials estimate the amounts of such transfers at $12–$15 million. While not an enormous flight of capital, the transfers helped diminish confidence in the island's economy.

Economic separatism between Cyprus and Greek and Turkish communities also gained momentum after 1957. Fanned by uncertainty over the island's political future and by the exhortations of extremists from both sides, a form of economic dualism developed. A Turkish-owned and -financed hotel was built in Ataturk Square in Nicosia; a Turkish-produced cola drink was introduced to compete with Pepsi-Cola and Coca-Cola, whose franchise owners are Greek Cypriotes; a boycott of Greek merchants by Turkish consumers rose and fell in intensity with shifts in the political climate.

Despite initial successes of the advocates of economic separatism, it did not sustain for long its early momentum.

There were several reasons for this: first, the Turkish community, largely agricultural or employed in government, quickly expended most of its funds for investment, and by mid-1960 new investment in separatist enterprises had dropped sharply; next, government officials from Turkey, on visits to Cyprus, were frequently outspoken in urging Turks to abandon economic separatism; third, the Greek business community began to abandon its occasional arrogance on the subject — typical were a series of thoughtful newspaper articles on the need for economic cooperation written in mid-1960 by Nicos Lanitis, a Greek Cypriote businessman; further, the construction of separate tax collection and expenditure arrangements seemed hard to enforce, even to the most ardent separatists; and finally those in economic authority in the new Republic have to date leaned over backwards to avoid favoritism to either community.

Despite the logical arguments against economic separatism, and the drop in its intensity after independence, it still remains a central problem facing the new Republic. Rooted completely in emotional and political arguments, it has no economic justification of any kind. Contemplation of the costs, administrative difficulties, and utter futility of separate facilities and economies for the island's Greek and Turkish communities is a melancholy task indeed.

A more hopeful development in republican Cyprus has been the appointment of an Economic Advisory Commission of top-level civil servants. Charged with blocking out a set of directions and magnitudes for public investment, the Commission as initially constituted combined a group of unusually well-informed and qualified members. Many problems remain, particularly with regard to the Commission's authority, its relationships with the presidency and the regular departments of government, the extent to which its functions are purely advisory or concerned with implementation of projects, and so on. Yet an able group has been appointed, and its members seem intent on seeking impartial advice, both from within the island and from outside. The Commission worked with a survey group sent by the United Nations Technical Assistance Board in 1960. The result was a highly useful set of "Suggestions for a Development Programme" published in 1961. The program envisioned expenditures of about $120 million over a five-year period.

The nature of the agreement between the Republic and the United Kingdom is also auspicious for Cyprus. Political considerations aside, the arrangement calls for grants for economic development from outside totaling about $40 million over the years 1960–1964. Thus $8 million yearly from outside is designed for development expenditure, largely under the aegis of the Cyprus government. The funds will doubtless be spent largely on public works and infrastructure projects. When these are added to development funds available from tax revenues of about $15 million yearly, a sizable development effort is made possible.

Of much more importance to Cyprus' economic welfare are the arrangements for troop quartering and military base operations. As contemplated in 1960, these called for stationing of more than 20,000 British troops and technicians on the island. Total capital transfers from the United Kingdom — for soldier and base-worker pay, improvement of installations and new military constructions, and the like — for so many troops could, on the basis of past performance, easily total $30 million yearly.

Still another hopeful feature, for the next several years at least, is the situation with regard to exports of Cyprus' mineral products. By substantial investments in facilities on the island and, more important, in new by-product processes and marketing facilities in Europe, the Cyprus Mines Corporation has to date kept the island's cupreous and iron pyrites, refined copper, and other marketable mineral products highly competitive in world markets. Despite recent world oversupply of such products, production has grown and tax-royalties paid to the Cyprus government each year have edged steadily upward. Yet depletion of high-grade ore bodies is imminent, and continuance of high earnings will depend on arrangements, involving constantly improving technology, to develop the island's poorer seams, as well as improvements in marketing and product usage in Europe.

For the next three to five years, therefore, Cyprus can look forward with reasonable certainty to capital transfers of more than $50 million yearly — roughly $40 million for troop quartering and base investments and $10 million in development grants from the United Kingdom. In addition, the island should earn at least $10 million yearly in tax-royalty from its mineral exports. Equal to more than 25 per cent of recent national income, these funds guarantee that the financial resources will be available to permit the Cypriote investor, if he will, to duplicate his extraordinary performance of the past decade. Using approximately equal transfers in recent years, he invested at the rate of 25 per cent of national income in many years after 1955.

Except for minerals, the job will be one essentially for the Cypriote investor, public and private, and not for the foreign private investor. Outside assistance from Greece and Turkey, moreover, will probably remain largely verbal. In 1960, Greece was granting about 150 scholarships for study in Athens to Cypriotes; Turkey had given a total of about $3 million to the Turkish community (for a cooperative credit scheme) and also was aiding the education of Turkish Cypriotes in various ways. In view of their own problems of economic development, Greece and Turkey will probably aid Cyprus in the future mainly in the field of education.

Also, with a little luck, Cyprus should have adequate funds to run its government and to maintain the order so necessary for the new nation's long-term prosperity. Present estimates call for expenditures of about $45 million yearly on government, with income arising as follows: customs taxes, $17,000,000; excise taxes, $6,000,000; income taxes, $10,000,000; miscellaneous income, $12,000,000.

Cyprus' economic future, therefore, looks hopeful for the first five years of nationhood. Yet the key question remains: can the government and Cypriote private investors undertake commitments which will speed changes in the basic structure of Cyprus' economy and in the composition of its national income — meanwhile creating a vehicle for sustained growth? Investment weighted heavily in urban housing and only lightly in agriculture, industry, and tourism will not trigger Cyprus into lasting prosperity, based on increased productivity all around and better use of resources. Nor will it right the unbalance of incomes now prevalent, with rural incomes still averaging only half those of urban dwellers.

Obviously the central economic problem facing Cyprus is that of the island's agriculture. As was made clear earlier, the Cypriote farmer is cursed by too little water, monotonously regular crop failures due to low rainfall, overfragmented holdings, an eroded topsoil, lack of mixed farming, low rural per capita income. And the island's industry, capital formation, capacity to consume, and general viability are closely linked to better rural conditions.

Under the circumstances, an attack on these problems can probably only be launched by the island's two main sources of funds and power — the government and the autocephalous Church. With United Kingdom funds available, the government should have sufficient resources for pilot reconsolidation schemes designed for the varying farming conditions on Cyprus. The Church, as the island's largest single landowner, controlling more than 8 per cent of the island's farmland, should be able to provide land for the experiments. More important, the Church might, once conclusive results are obtained, be more effective than the government in persuading peasants to agree to consolidation and soil improvement programs. In this respect, the peculiar relation between Church and State in Cyprus offers reasons for qualified hope.

But improved land use and tenure are not enough. More water must be found. Well drilling experiments have not proved dramatically successful, and the island's measurable water table is generally agreed to be dropping at an alarming rate. Recent studies have concluded that great improvements in systems of collecting winter rain and snow runoff, employing new earth-compacting techniques, are still practicable. Probably well drilling will, and must, continue. Until more natural water is found, however (or until ways are found to check runoff and evaporation), Cyprus will share nearby Israel's plight of having to look toward scientific and technological breakthroughs which will make sea water distillation economically practicable. In the interim (the same one occupied by most of the underdeveloped world) preceding the advent of adequate water supplies, the Cyprus government must maintain the momentum gained by United Kingdom experiments on the island with low-rainfall grasses, weedicides (which in effect eliminate weeds as a thirsty competitor to productive crops for water), covered irrigation ditches, catchment plans, and the other elements in a system of water conservation.

Improvement of industry is clearly the second major economic task facing independent Cyprus. As shown earlier, the

Cyprus Mines Corporation and three or four bottling plants — including Pepsi-Cola and Coca-Cola — are the only industrial ventures whose productivity and general efficiency make them competitive on international standards. Cost of production in most Cyprus factories is much higher than in Holland, and the average industrial worker produces a third as much as does the German worker. The strong trade union movement creates a cost-push which joins with poor entrepreneurship, lack of local raw materials, high power costs, and a narrow domestic market to make it virtually impossible for Cyprus factories to add value (without subsidy) and compete in markets abroad.

Since the problems of industry seem very complicated and, in the eyes of some, the hardest to solve, and since the island's industry ranges across a broad spectrum — from household lace making to mineral production — some feel that the government's first task should be to conduct a broad-scale industrial feasibility study. This could be modeled after those undertaken recently in many underdeveloped countries and would be designed to seek new ventures and to improve those already established. Such a study, aimed at creating import-substitute industries as well as exporting industries, might add to the highly useful beginning outlined in the recent United Nations report.

One source of earnings which obviously could stand improvement is tourism. During the emergency, tourism dwindled to virtually nothing. In 1960, for example, Cyprus had yet to begin a really vigorous advertising campaign abroad, it offered no special exchange rates to bona fide tourists, there was no program under way to build attractive small hotels or motels near the beautiful bays and beaches which dot the island's shoreline, there were no organized programs of summer music and drama festivals, no gambling casinos, no all-out effort to improve and publicize the mountain ski resort facilities. While ill-conceived investments could prove wasteful, much could be done to improve Cyprus' earnings from this source.

In the commercial and financial sector, the government presumably will consider pushing the Cyprus merchant into the East-West entrepôt trade and broadening his activities in international banking and finance. Better airport and deep-water port facilities could, if plans are completed, give the island such physical facilities as free zone warehouses, more frequent arrivals and departures of planes and vessels. But the island's commercial success or failure will really depend on the agility of the Cypriote merchant as he nears for the first time the whirring knives of a less sheltered economy.

Cyprus' economic future will also, in the near future at least, be influenced by its skill in walking the tightrope of neutrality between nearby Arab states and Israel. At the moment the island's economy needs, and gets, tourists from both sides; Cyprus is a stopover point for tourists visiting the Arab States and Israel; it gains some income from providing an open-ended keyhole through which peer the military intelligence operators from both sides; it exports wines and goat cheese to several Arab countries. Yet Cyprus may in the future profit from Israeli technical assistance or from low-cost imports — subsidized for Israeli exporters by American Jewry. It is already a loophole in the Arab blockade against Israel. Several Arab states, meanwhile, consider British bases on Cyprus as directed primarily against them. Given these conflicting forces, Cyprus' economic neutrality will be difficult to maintain.

The government also will face, in this connection, problems of monetary and credit policy. It has decided for an initial ten-year membership in the sterling area. But a separate

Cyprus bank of issue is practically certain, and lending institutions following rules laid down by the Cyprus government (and not the United Kingdom Treasury) already operate. The government will certainly face the usual arguments for and against inflationary finance.

A final problem is worth mentioning. That is the seemingly inevitable one facing new and old states on this planetload of warring tribes — the competition between funds for economic development and those for military expenditure. Serious talk of a Cypriote army, 2,000 men strong and costing an estimated $6 million yearly to sustain, has gone on since the Zurich agreement built an army into the Constitution for the island. One can only express the hope that if the Republic fields an army, it will design it from the beginning as a training program in literacy, skills, and crafts of various kinds, and hence as an aid to economic development. To concentrate on purely military matters at this juncture would seem the essence of waste and folly.

To cope with all these problems, the Cyprus Planning Commission unquestionably must try, as mentioned many times earlier, to speed change in the island's economic structure. And it must do so in full realization that Cyprus cannot yet qualify, despite its impressive figures of national-income growth, reinvestment, and literacy, for membership in the exclusive coterie of underdeveloped nations said by economists to be in the "take-off" stage. Excessive dependence on the outside world is still central to the island's economic welfare. A shift in British cold war strategy could overnight leave the economy of Cyprus stalled dismally at the end of the runway.

The new government's major economic task in the next five years, therefore, is to guarantee the outside sources of financial support. If these outside pillars of sustenance remain erect, the Planning Commission's work may, with luck, develop into more than a wild gambler's throw.

The short-term pillars, of course, are: first, troop quartering, which affords fields for the Cyprus private investor and remains the island's principal source of economic vitality; second, mineral exports, which pay for a third of the government payroll, provide sizable employment, and can — by proper government encouragement to firms intent on working low-grade ore bodies — be kept at reasonably high levels; third, maintenance of British Commonwealth status or other guarantees for the safety valve of emigration — permitting movement abroad of two to three thousand Cypriotes yearly, with resultant releases of social pressures and transfer back to the island of remittances earned abroad; finally, an immediate and vigorous effort to increase earnings from tourism.

Cyprus' short-term economic future, therefore, is hopeful. Its long-term chances depend on the extent to which its human resources can develop, and in the process change the nature of the economy. The wisdom of its government for the next few years will be crucial. Cyprus has a rare chance, with its unique location, small population, and past record of growth, to attract even greater outside resources than it now enjoys — from the United Nations, from new technical and economic assistance programs being blueprinted in Europe, and possibly from the United States. One hopes that the energies which made the island politically independent may be channeled into enduring economic development.

Appendix

Structural Interdependence: An Input-Output View

As noted earlier, Cyprus is a rare underdeveloped country in that it offers abundant economic data to the student of its past ten years of economic expansion. Its national income, its balance of payments, and similar information are well, and fairly accurately, known. Yet these data, while highly useful, go only part-way toward providing a complete x-ray of the economy. They do not show, for example, how the various sectors (agriculture, industry, trade, finance, and government) relate to one another in actual buying and selling terms. They give only a slight indication of the extent to which mutually complementary, self-generating agricultural and industrial revolutions are under way, in which increased rural and urban productivity and purchasing power feed one another.

To assess better the nature of these revolutions on Cyprus, and to inquire further if the island's economy has indeed entered the "take-off" stage indicated by its relatively high (and rapidly increasing) per capita income, literacy rate, and levels of investment during the 1950's, the authors of this study set about to measure the changes with an input-output accounting system. A sophisticated method of analysis, designed originally for use in the industrial countries of the West, input-output accounts represent a form of double entry bookkeeping based on the transactions of all producer and consumer units in the economy. The data are placed in tables which record transactions between sectors of the economy and provide a checkerboard accounting showing graphically the outputs (sales) and the inputs (purchases) of each sector.

Two tables were constructed for Cyprus, for the years 1954 and 1957. These years served as terminal dates for the simple reason that they marked the earliest and latest periods for which the necessary data were available. Similar studies done on the economies of England and America have, for a variety of reasons, covered a somewhat longer time span. The years 1954–1957, it should also be noted, were years of political emergency on Cyprus.

The Cyprus tables, shown in Appendix Charts A and B, contain a total of 105 rows. The stub contains a list of producing sectors and the column heads show the destination of goods generated by the producing sectors. Items 1–18 portray selling and buying within the agriculture sector, items 19–61, manufacturing and related ventures, items 62–95, imports; the remaining categories portray the role of commerce, transport, and government.

From the two major tables, a set of condensed portrayals became possible. These included, first, a simplified interindustry flow of goods and services by industry of origin and destination for the years in question; next, a breakdown showing sales to other industries, domestic final demand, and exports; third, a breakdown of the quantity of output going to industry, for domestic demand, and to export for the sectors of agriculture and industry; finally, a charting of the degree of direct influence exerted by each industry upon the prospects of other industries.

The major conclusion to be drawn from the input-output charts is that alluded to earlier, namely that the degree of intersectoral economic linkage on Cyprus is slight. Food and beverage industries alone draw much of their raw material inputs from the island's agriculture — and interdependence grew sharply during the four-year span. But except for this, buying and selling between sectors is relatively unimportant. Buying and selling within the industrial sector, moreover, from one factory to another, is also slight. The role of imports in the economy is great — probably too great.

The next general conclusion to be drawn from the charts is that, except for growth in the flow of agricultural products into food and beverage factories, there was little shift in the sectoral relationships over the four-year period. Cyprus industry decreased its dependence on imports only slightly and likewise stepped up its buying and selling from other industries on the island only slightly. The main evidence of shift during the period was one of transfer from government to household purchasing.

Besides showing graphically the lack of related self-generating industrial and agricultural development on Cyprus, the input-output tables also show, in more detailed form, the data already available from import-export accounts and other measures of the island's economic performance. They show in considerable detail where imports go on Cyprus, the contribution of the various crops and commodities to exports, and the heavy role played by mining and government in the island's economy.

In addition to making possible the conclusions mentioned, the tables might also prove useful to those charged with setting a new economic course for Cyprus during its first decade of independence. The tables show dramatically the holes to be filled. Should the holes be filled and more sectoral linkage develop, it might be possible — employing numerical coefficients and linear programming techniques used by input-output specialists — to trace through the economy, and perhaps forecast with better accuracy than is now possible, the effects of investment in one sector or industry on investment and output in other sectors. Such an exercise was not the task of this study, but might, if the technique develops further, prove of service in the future.

Bibliographical Note

The tables and charts in this book, unless otherwise noted, were produced by the Statistics Section of the Crown Colony's Financial Secretary's Office — now the Finance Ministry of the Republic of Cyprus. Only a few footnote references are included, because most of the tables appear in the annual issues of the *Cyprus Economic Review*. Since the book is designed primarily for American readers, pounds have been converted to dollars.

A highly useful reference work is the recently completed *Cyprus — Suggestions for a Development Programme* (United Nations, 1961). Written by Professor Willard Thorp and a team of United Nations Technical Assistance Board experts, the study resulted from a several months' inquiry on the island in the autumn of 1960.

Economists interested in application of the input-output techniques to Cyprus are referred to Simos Vassiliou, *Input-Output Analysis of the Economy of Cyprus* (offset print manuscript, Harvard Center for Middle Eastern Studies, 1959). Distillation of material in this study is contained in the Appendix to the present volume.

Since 1950, the government of Cyprus has published a mass of data of direct and indirect relevance to the island's economy. Most notable are the *Monthly Statistical Summaries* (which include information on migration, trade, finance, and production); the annual reports of the various government departments (particularly useful are those of the Finance, Commerce and Industries, and Agriculture departments); and the Cyprus annual *Report*. In addition to the foregoing, the authors made use of much unpublished material, and several reports in the archives of the Crown Colony financial Secretariat.

A document of great economic as well as political significance to Cyprus is the volume containing the London and Zurich agreements and the Constitution of the Republic, agreed upon during lengthy meetings in 1959 and 1960. This volume is *Cyprus* (London: H. M. Stationery Office, 1960).

A source of interpretative material during the 1950's was the Cyprus Federation of Trade and Industry. It employed consultants to produce memoranda of various kinds. Among these were two studies by P. T. Bauer and B. S. Yamey, *Aspects of Government Intervention in Co-operation and Agricultural Marketing in Cyprus* (Nicosia, 1955) and *The Economics of the Vine Products Scheme in Cyprus* (Nicosia, 1955).

A comprehensive account of the origins and nature of Cyprus' land problem may be found in Demetris Christodolou, *The Evolution of the Rural Land Use Pattern in Cyprus* (Bude, Cornwall, England, 1959).

Few of the books on recent events in Cyprus are useful to the student of its economy. Most devote themselves to a defense of one of the several sides in the recent political troubles, and are little more than political tracts. An exception is Laurence Durrell's *Bitter Lemons* (London, 1957).

Index

HARVARD MIDDLE EASTERN STUDIES

1. *Desert Enterprise: The Middle East Oil Industry in Its Local Environment,* by David H. Finnie, 1958.
2. *Middle Eastern Capitalism: Nine Essays,* by A. J. Meyer, 1959.
3. *The Idea of the Jewish State,* by Ben Halpern, 1961.
4. *The Agricultural Policy of Muhammad 'Alī in Egypt,* by Helen Anne B. Rivlin, 1961.
5. *Egypt in Search of Political Community,* by Nadav Safran, 1961.
6. *The Economy of Cyprus,* by A. J. Meyer, with Simos Vassiliou, 1962.

BOOKS FROM THE CENTER FOR INTERNATIONAL AFFAIRS

PUBLISHED BY HARVARD UNIVERSITY PRESS

The Soviet Bloc, by Zbigniew K. Brzezinski, 1960 (jointly with the Russian Research Center).

Rift and Revolt in Hungary, by Ferenc A. Váli, 1961.

The Economy of Cyprus, by A. J. Meyer, with Simos Vassiliou, 1962.

PUBLISHED BY OTHERS

The Necessity for Choice, by Henry A. Kissinger, 1961. Harper & Brothers.

Strategy and Arms Control, by Thomas C. Schelling and Morton H. Halperin, 1961. Twentieth Century Fund.

United States Manufacturing Investment in Brazil, by Lincoln Gordon and Engelbert L. Grommers, 1962. Harvard Business School.

APPENDIX CHART A
(over for Chart B)

PRODUCING

		1	2	3	4	5	6	7	8	9	10	11	12	13	14
		CEREALS	LEGUMES	GREEN FODDER CROP	POTATOES	INDUSTRIAL CROPS	AROMATIC CROPS	TOBACCO	ONIONS	VEGETABLES	CITRUS FRUIT	MELONS	GRAPES	OLIVES	CAROBS
	AGRICULTURE														
1	CEREALS	1781		78											
2	LEGUMES		196												
3	GREEN FODDER CROPS														
4	POTATOES				109										
5	INDUSTRIAL CROPS					14									
6	AROMATIC CROPS						1								
7	TOBACCO														
8	ONIONS								14						
9	VEGETABLES														
10	CITRUS FRUIT														
11	MELONS														
12	GRAPES														
13	OLIVES														
14	CAROBS														
15	OTHER FRUITS & NUTS														
16	LIVESTOCK	28	3	3	6			3	3	11	42	3		42	
17	FORESTRY FISH. & HUNT														
18	OTHER AGRICULTURE														
	MINING & QUARRYING														
19	METAL MINING														
20	STONE QUARRYING														
21	NON-METALLIC MINING														
	MAN. INDUSTRIES														
22	MEAT PRESERVING														
23	DAIRY PRODUCTS														
24	FRUIT & VEG. CANNING														
25	GRAIN MILL PRODUCTS														
26	BAKERY PRODUCTS														
27	SUGAR CONFECTIONERY														
28	OTHER FOOD INDUSTRIES														
29	ALCOHOLIC DRINKS														
30	SOFT DRINKS														
31	TOBACCO MANUFACTURES														
32	TEXTILES														
33	FOOTWEAR														
34	WEARING APPAREL														
35	MADE UP TEX. GOODS														
36	WOOD & CORK MAN.														
37	FURNITURE & FIXTURES														
38	PAPER GOODS														
39	PRINTING & PUBLISHING														
40	TANNING														
41	LEATHER GOODS														
42	RUBBER GOODS														
43	VEG. OILS & FATS														
44	CHEMICAL PRODUCTS														
45	BUILDING MATERIALS														

INTERINDUSTRY FLOW OF
BY INDUSTRY OF ORIGIN AND

(ALL FIGURES IN THO

INDUSTRY

15 OTHER FRUITS & NUTS	16 LIVESTOCK	17 FORESTRY FISH. & HUN	18 OTHER AGRICULTURE	19 METAL MINING	20 STONE QUARRYING	21 NON-METALLIC MINING	22 MEAT PRESERVING	23 DAIRY PRODUCTS	24 FRUIT & VEG. CANNING	25 GRAIN MILL PRODUCTS	26 BAKERY PRODUCTS	27 SUGAR CONFECTIONERY	28 OTHER FOOD INDUST.	29 ALCOHOLIC DRINKS	30 SOFT DRINKS	31 TOBACCO MANUFAC.	32 TEXTILES	33 FOOTWEAR	34 WEARING APPAREL
	2755									4900									
	652																		
	2588																		
																	143		
																39			
									92										
															616				
														2851	61				
													1999						
													2402						
									213			30							
3							650	1210											
													263						
	104										7851		294						
	28						6		4										
																			109
																		400	

GOODS AND SERVICES
DESTINATION 1954

OUSAND OF DOLLARS)

PURCHASING

	35 MADE UP TEX. GOODS	36 WOOD & CORK MAN.	37 FURNITURE & FIXTU.	38 PAPER GOODS	39 PRINTING & PUBLIS.	40 TANNING	41 LEATHER GOODS	42 RUBBER GOODS	43 VEG. OILS & FATS	44 CHEMICAL PRODUCTS	45 BUILDING MATERIAL	46 GLASS PRODUCTS	47 NON-METALLIC PRO.	48 METAL PROD. N.E.S.	49 MACHINERY N.E.S.	50 ELECTRIC MACHIN.	51 SHIP BUILDING	52 MOTOR CAR REP.	53 BICYCLE REPAIRS	54 TRANSPORT EQUIP.
									112											
						53														
		780																		
											1140		411							
									140											
3																				
			662																	
										177										

55 CLOCKS & WATCHES	56 JEWELLERY	57 MUSICAL INSTRUM.	58 OTHER INDUSTRIES	59 CONSTRUCTION	60 ELECTRICITY	61 WATER	62 EXPORTS	96 COMMERCE	97 TRANSPORT	98 SERVICES	99 UNDISTRIBUTIVE	100 GOVERNMENT	101 INVENTORY	102 GROSS CAPITAL FOR.	103 HOUSEHOLDS	105 GROSS OUTPUT
							930					1190			423	12057
							235								928	2011
																2588
							2621								1653	4383
							367									636
							210								3	214
							314									353
							230								42	286
							204								2156	2452
							3592							448	420	5076
							154								557	711
							1506							6	185	4609
														3		2002
							118							8		2528
							400							6	1344	1993
							963								16828	19851
							64								633	1477
							45								932	977
							24144							560		24704
				468												468
							2668							132		4614
													3		921	924
							350						11		1515	1876
							45								425	470
													8		20	8277
							14						148		8313	8475
							132						42		347	521
							3264						128		2528	6098
							1305								4514	5819
							90						193		2004	2287
															4794	4794
							70						143			1311
							56						104		2800	2960
															9117	9117
							25						23		909	957
															442	1104
				1526									64		1910	3500
							3								25	28
												129	3		1097	1229
							174						20			594
															36	36
									50						48	98
							98								196	471
													14		344	358
				2302												2302

INDUSTRY P

46	GLASS PRODUCTS														
47	NON-METALLIC PRODUCTS														
48	METAL PRODUCTS N.E.S.														
49	MACHINERY N.E.S.	45		14						12	26				
50	ELECTRIC MACHINERY														
51	SHIP BUILDING														
52	MOTOR-CAR REPAIRS														
53	BICYCLE REPAIRS														
54	TRANSPORT EQUIPMENT														
55	CLOCKS & WATCHES														
56	JEWELLERY														
57	MUSICAL INSTRUMENTS														
58	OTHER INDUSTRIES														
59	CONSTRUCTION	28			6					6	11				
60	ELECTRICITY														
61	WATER														
	IMPORTS														
62	LIVESTOCK & MEAT														
63	DAIRY PRODUCTS														
64	FISH & FISH PRODUCTS														
65	CEREALS ETC.	8													
66	FRUITS & NUTS														
67	SUGAR & SUGAR PREP.														
68	FEEDING ST. FOR ANIMAL														
69	VEG. OILS AND FATS														
70	OTHER FOOD														
71	ALCOHOLIC BEVERAGES														
72	TOBACCO UNMANUFACTURED														
73	TOBACCO MANUFACTURED														
74	HIDES & SKINS														
75	OIL SEEDS														
76	WOOD & MANUFACTURES										532	14	22		
77	FUELS & LUBRICANTS	56		6	6					3	56	6			
78	CHEMICALS & MANUFAC														
79	DYES ETC.														
80	ESSENTIAL OILS ETC.														
81	FERTILIZERS ETC.	1283		6	196	1	2	1	1	49	78	33	50		
82	LEATHER GOODS														
83	RUBBER GOODS														
84	PAPER GOODS										165				
85	TEXTILE YARNS														
86	TEXTILE FABRICS														
87	TEXTILE GOODS														
88	CEMENT														
89	CONSTRUCTION MATERIALS														
90	TRANSPORT EQUIPMENT														
91	PIPES TUBES ETC.														
92	MACHINERY														
93	CLOTHING														
94	FOOTWEAR														
95	OTHER				627			3			14				
96	COMMERCE	168			8						168				
97	TRANSPORT	42	14	3	179					28	608	22	160		45
98	SERVICES	168		17	42					14	28	3	20	6	5
99	UNDISTRIBUTIVE														
100	GOVERNMENT	426	6	64	32					3	174	2	98	34	98
101	INVENTORY							104	34				882		
102	GROSS CAPITAL FORMATION														
103	HOUSEHOLDS	2100	3	202	442	3	3	3	11	125	1056	56	504	188	294
104	VALUE ADDED	5924	1789	2195	2729	618	208	239	223	2201	2118	572	2873	1732	2086
105	GROSS OUTLAY	12057	2011	2588	4383	636	214	353	286	2452	5076	711	4609	2002	2528

																			30	
		11	14		19		3													
																	11			
		39																		
		64									2716									
													82		22	42				
		126																		
																	470			
															190	14			14	
	6		14	3	90	9	13	1	3	2	6	21	1		28	112	42	3		
					112					2						14				
															45	70				
	14			3																
																			686	
																			39	
																	45			
																		608		
																				451
									1	1		17	203	15	48	64				
		330									84				70	106	48	17	188	1235
	14	157	14	3	498	12	78		34		42	39	6	90	140	20	3	3	14	5
	3	196			95	5	12		14		56	21		16	42	28	3	48	8	143
	3	77	3	2	6900		100		8		28	8			431	17	3545	17	126	557
					563										308	34	81			
	120	2078	28	140	3279	176	1101	20	50	5	117	218	118	249	418	252	188	174	597	350
5	1830	10646	1404	826	13148	266	3307	247	556	151	328	300	81	770	1226	837	319	298	858	1212
3	1993	19851	1477	977	24704	468	4614	924	1876	470	8277	8475	521	6098	5819	2287	4794	1311	2960	911

		17																		
			3																	
			7		8										13			15		
										39										
						143														
									123											
			1120														11			73
		11	4		1	8			3		6		8							
						14							4							
			157			28							3							
										14										
							14													
								28												
				22	280															
3	518																			
		9	8		55							16		336	200	14		112	56	3
	129		353			22		6		17	3			48	20			22	11	15
	3	25	34		8	3		3	3	6	42		53	8						
	11		364						6	6	48			5	8			4	1	
	6		115		10	22		6												2
											48									
	14	148	294	3	423	34	6	22	56	39	370	14	232	174	199	25	22	339	17	34
	276	114	379	3	444	267	16	33	28	60	645	15	386	459	72	14	9	166	100	47
7	957	1104	3500	28	1229	594	36	98	471	358	2302	45	1097	1030	512	53	42	658	185	174

															45	45
				894			193						10			1097
				468											562	1030
															368	512
									22						31	53
														42		42
									60						598	658
															185	185
														174		174
															50	50
															140	140
															2	2
							493						12		481	986
					3			28				266	134	22218	4845	27595
										28		26			1755	1863
															504	504
							39								267	345
							176								846	1022
							39								445	484
							45								507	3340
							11								792	803
															484	630
																126
							56								1548	1643
							314								593	907
							42								143	185
																470
							64								409	473
																143
																123
				841			8								224	3063
			6		165	25			2422						2739	5885
							8								691	845
				280			11								11	490
															734	863
																1717
																700
							3		720	20						810
				141											537	1190
							25									633
																5031
							67								1355	1422
				1560												1560
				2811												2811
							381		336					2990	1588	5295
				1280												1280
							305							6790		7095
							20						(-336)		3116	2800
															644	644
6	34		420				854	70		400			(-1078)	1767	8571	12846
1	7		21	742					560		3	308		2276	14613	21602
			5	669	1			3304	28	2316	28	840			7113	16766
			8	280	252			1912	140	137		2741			14080	20996
															4200	4200
1	5			448				560	1210	325					16177	31646
																2054
8	20	1	297	8254	417	87		3512	5636	5110	4169	14000			462	59106
34	74	1	229	4631	1025	392		12216	5582	12660						104494
50	140	2	986	27595	1863	504	47545	21602	16766	20996	4200	19500	(-354)	37420	160864	521071

APPENDIX CHART B
(over for Chart A)

		1	2	3	4	5	6	7	8	9	10	11	12	13	14
		CEREALS	LEGUMES	GREEN FODDER CROPS	POTATOES	INDUSTRIAL CROPS	AROMATIC CROPS	TOBACCO	ONIONS	VEGETABLES	CITRUS FRUIT	MELONS	GRAPES	OLIVES	CAROBS
	AGRICULTURE														
1	CEREALS	1845		78											
2	LEGUMES		215	213											
3	GREEN FODDER CROPS														
4	POTATOES				98										
5	INDUSTRIAL CROPS					12									
6	AROMATIC CROPS						1								
7	TOBACCO														
8	ONIONS								12						
9	VEGETABLES														
10	CITRUS FRUIT														
11	MELONS														
12	GRAPES														
13	OLIVES														
14	CAROBS														
15	OTHER FRUITS & NUTS														
16	LIVESTOCK	31	3	7	8			3	3	21	56	4		70	
17	FORESTRY FISH. & HUNT														
18	OTHER AGRICULTURE														
	MINING & QUARRYING														
19	METAL MINING														
20	STONE QUARRYING														
21	NON-METALLIC MINING														
	MAN. INDUSTRIES														
22	MEAT PRESERVING														
23	DAIRY PRODUCTS														
24	FRUIT & VEG. CANNING														
25	GRAIN MILL PRODUCTS														
26	BAKERY PRODUCTS														
27	SUGAR CONFECTIONERY														
28	OTHER FOOD INDUSTRIES														
29	ALCOHOLIC DRINKS														
30	SOFT DRINKS														
31	TOBACCO MANUFACTURES														
32	TEXTILES														
33	FOOTWEAR														
34	WEARING APPAREL														
35	MADE UP TEX. GOODS														
36	WOOD & CORK MAN.														
37	FURNITURE & FIXTURES														
38	PAPER GOODS														
39	PRINTING & PUBLISHING														
40	TANNING														
41	LEATHER GOODS														
42	RUBBER GOODS														
43	VEG. OILS & FATS														
44	CHEMICAL PRODUCTS														
45	BUILDING MATERIALS														

RODUCING

INTERINDUSTRY FLOW OF

BY INDUSTRY OF ORIGIN AND

(ALL FIGURES IN TH

INDUSTRY

15 OTHER FRUITS & NUTS	16 LIVESTOCK	17 FORESTRY FISH. & HUN	18 OTHER AGRICULTURE	19 METAL MINING	20 STONE QUARRYING	21 NON-METALLIC MINING	22 MEAT PRESERVING	23 DAIRY PRODUCTS	24 FRUIT & VEG. CANNING	25 GRAIN MILL PRODUCTS	26 BAKERY PRODUCTS	27 SUGAR CONFECTIONERY	28 OTHER FOOD INDUSTRY	29 ALCOHOLIC DRINKS	30 SOFT DRINKS	31 TOBACCO MANUFAC.	32 TEXTILES	33 FOOTWEAR	34 WEARING APPAREL
	2844									4844									
	1002																		
	6163																		
																	294		
																204			
									286										
															925				
														3091	137				
													2831						
													2402						
									420			30							
4							830	1880											
													263						
	120										8323		382						
	45						7		6										
																			170
																		450	

G O O D S   A N D   S E R V I C E S

D E S T I N A T I O N   1 9 5 7

OUSAND OF DOLLARS)

P U R C H A S I N G

	35 MADE UP TEX. GOODS	36 WOOD & CORK MAN.	37 FURNITURE & FIXTURES	38 PAPER GOODS	39 PRINTING & PUBLISH.	40 TANNING	41 LEATHER GOODS	42 RUBBER GOODS	43 VEG. OILS & FATS	44 CHEMICAL PRODUCTS	45 BUILDING MATERIALS	46 GLASS PRODUCTS	47 NON-METALLIC PRO.	48 METAL PROD. N.E.S.	49 MACHINERY N.E.S.	50 ELECTRIC MACHINERY	51 SHIP BUILDING	52 MOTOR CAR REPAIRS	53 BICYCLE REPAIRS	54 TRANSPORT EQUIP.
									18											
						80														
		400																		
											1482		493							
									197											
4																				
			252																	
										215										

55 CLOCKS & WATCHES	56 JEWELLERY	57 MUSICAL INSTRUM.	58 OTHER INDUSTRIES	59 CONSTRUCTION	60 ELECTRICITY	61 WATER	62 EXPORTS	96 COMMERCE	97 TRANSPORT	98 SERVICES	99 UNDISTRIBUTIVE	100 GOVERNMENT	101 INVENTORY	102 GROSS CAPITAL FOR.	103 HOUSEHOLDS	105 GROSS OUTPUT
							1742					1915			430	13698
							106								788	2324
																6163
							1770								1727	3595
			14				14						132			484
							101								3	105
							552									756
							14						152		46	224
							160								2791	3237
							4900							1211	437	7473
							168								705	873
							2072					201		15	192	5708
														10		2841
							56							20		2478
							179							12	1314	1955
							618								22700	26318
							84								823	1307
							76								1044	1120
							26916							560		27476
				502												502
							2276							132		4646
															1155	1155
							280						441		1969	2690
							624								637	1261
																8828
							11								9115	9126
							95								463	558
							2484						643		3658	7040
							1862								4770	6632
							48								4722	4770
													341		4601	4942
													160			1864
							31						180		3039	3250
															11268	11268
							162								1618	1780
															480	732
				1610									200		3138	4948
															36	36
												218			1368	1586
							412									862
													5		80	85
									78						70	148
							179						215		320	929
															491	491
				2932									1500			4432

P INDUSTRY

46	GLASS PRODUCTS														
47	NON-METALLIC PRODUCTS														
48	METAL PRODUCTS N.E.S.														
49	MACHINERY N.E.S.	53		20						29	32				
50	ELECTRIC MACHINERY														
51	SHIP BUILDING														
52	MOTOR-CAR REPAIRS														
53	BICYCLE REPAIRS														
54	TRANSPORT EQUIPMENT														
55	CLOCKS & WATCHES														
56	JEWELLERY														
57	MUSICAL INSTRUMENTS														
58	OTHER INDUSTRIES			6											
59	CONSTRUCTION	42			8					9	14				
60	ELECTRICITY														
61	WATER														
	IMPORTS														
62	LIVESTOCK & MEAT														
63	DAIRY PRODUCTS														
64	FISH & FISH PRODUCTS														
65	CEREALS ETC.														
66	FRUITS & NUTS														
67	SUGAR & SUGAR PREP.														
68	FEEDING ST. FOR ANIM.														
69	VEG. OILS AND FATS														
70	OTHER FOOD														
71	ALCOHOLIC BEVERAGES														
72	TOBACCO UNMANUFACTURED														
73	TOBACCO MANUFACTURED														
74	HIDES & SKINS														
75	OIL SEEDS														
76	WOOD & MANUFACTURES										468	16	19		
77	FUELS & LUBRICANTS	101		21	7					5	70	8			
78	CHEMICALS & MANUFAC.														
79	DYES ETC.														
80	ESSENTIAL OILS ETC.														
81	FERTILIZERS ETC.	2600		13	372	1	1	1	1	58	117	42	80	10	
82	LEATHER GOODS														
83	RUBBER GOODS														
84	PAPER GOODS										347				
85	TEXTILE YARNS														
86	TEXTILE FABRICS														
87	TEXTILE GOODS														
88	CEMENT														
89	CONSTRUCTION MATERIALS														
90	TRANSPORT EQUIPMENT														
91	PIPES TUBES ETC.														
92	MACHINERY														
93	CLOTHING														
94	FOOTWEAR														
95	OTHER		87		448			5		22	18				
96	COMMERCE	312			8					1	244				
97	TRANSPORT	46	18	5	185					41	810	28	192		45
98	SERVICES	168		21	45					17	39	4	25	7	5
99	UNDISTRIBUTIVE														
100	GOVERNMENT	426	6	64	32					3	200	3	98	34	98
101	INVENTORY							350					1088		
102	GROSS CAPITAL FORMATION														
103	HOUSEHOLDS	1786	3	210	481	3	3	3	11	150	2125	87	444	170	305
104	VALUE ADDED	6288	1992	5505	1983	468	100	394	197	2881	2933	681	3762	2550	2025
105	GROSS OUTLAY	13698	2324	6163	3595	484	105	756	224	3237	7473	873	5708	2841	2478

																		30	
	11	14		25		4													
									4							11			
	8																		
	412									3192									
									36										
									9			82		26	81				
	255																		
																686			
														201	29			17	
8		16	3	118	13	16	2	5		7	25	1		32	195	42	5		
				121					2										
														52	154				
17			5																
																		708	
																		45	
									2							45			
																	879		
																			540
								2	53		19	203	21	60	119				1
	410									96				73	207	55	29	192	153
16	192	16	5	604	19	81		50	5	53	48	7	108	151	61	4	5	17	8
4	217			97	7	12		16		65	21		18	43	30	3	51	9	18
3	80	3	2	8946		95		8	3	28	8			890	38	3402	18	128	66
															350				
108	1829	35	140	3666	264	1222	27	62	106	146	293	138	265	543	452	195	226	711	42
1795	12722	1223	965	13899	199	3216	289	667	329	394	389	97	750	1470	1992	295	357	943	133
1955	26310	1307	1120	27476	502	4646	1155	2690	1261	8825	9126	558	7040	6632	4770	4942	1864	3250	1126

		15																		
			4																	
			11		10										18			20		
			34							104										
						120														
									582											
			2148														11			8
		10	8		1	8			4		24		10							
						14							5							
			297			28							3							
										18										
							51													
				29				53												
					352						294									
0	1100																			
5		9	11		67					2	20	19		512	305	19		213	65	
9	244		594			20	5	11		18	79			76	31			43	13	1
1	5	25	41		14	4		4	5	8	339		65	10						
0	15		425						7	8	85			7	9			7	1	
9	8		150		12	19		11												
						254														
0	18	163	390	4	550	40	8	27	67	51	524	18	278	209	242	31	24	453	21	4
3	390	110	583	3	580	275	21	42	49	67	1585	16	427	506	98	16	9	302	105	4
8	1780	732	4948	36	1586	862	85	148	929	491	4432	53	1281	1320	703	66	44	1038	205	19

																53	53
					990									291			1281
					618											702	1320
																524	703
										28						38	66
															44		44
										114						924	1038
																205	205
															124	75	199
																43	43
																226	226
																2	2
								361						218		433	1018
						5			42				1464		28560	7402	37604
											50		85			4822	5031
																731	731
																2117	2125
								14								2089	2103
																809	809
								3								1444	5051
								8								1482	1526
								3						314		1215	1730
																	255
																1886	2024
														110		1993	2103
								59								1548	1607
																6	692
								22						85		3819	3926
																	120
																	582
5					1127			22						200		263	4606
				8		495	55	1165		3839						6015	12342
								22						50		1441	1655
					520			3								14	865
								6								1685	1915
														154			3472
																	759
								14		1630	34			(−97)			1708
					70			8						165		809	2092
																	879
														783			7283
								31								1277	1308
					1285												1285
					3360												3360
								1207		420					6163	2699	10489
					2394												2394
								272							14555		14827
								28								4836	4864
								3								1669	1672
5	8	65		434				1635	180		655				2612	15446	23354
8	1	13		23	989					948		5	921		3500	23753	34471
				7	936	5			7929	51	4400	49	2112			8343	27172
				9	364	592			5780	287	180		3563			15323	27766
																5600	5600
3	1	8			597				815	2747	408					25541	45605
																	2042
1	9	38	1	342	14132	1501	170		5286	7408	6863	5546	36820			560	98384
7	24	102	1	181	5178	2433	506		14439	9622	15176						127976
9	43	226	2	1018	37604	5031	731	52878	34471	27172	27766	5600	47299	6242	57518	235860	737055

Bei Fragen zur Produktsicherheit wenden Sie sich bitte an:
If you have any questions regarding product safety,
please contact:

Walter de Gruyter GmbH
Genthiner Straße 13
10785 Berlin
productsafety@degruyterbrill.com